WARRIOR
WITHOUT WEAPONS

An Army Medic's Life aboard the *Queen Mary* during World War II

WARRIOR
WITHOUT WEAPONS

An Army Medic's Life aboard the *Queen Mary* during World War II

by
Robert R. Copeland

edited by
Martine H. Justak

GRIFFING-HORNE PRESS, INC. Indianapolis, Indiana

WARRIOR WITHOUT WEAPONS

Cover Design by Connie Staggs

Library of Congress Cataloging-in-Publication Data

Copeland, Robert R., 1918-1988
    Warrior without weapons : an Army medic's life aboard the Queen Mary during World War II / by Robert R. Copeland ; edited by Martine H. Justak.
        p. cm.
ISBN 0-9622964-0-6
1. Copeland, Robert R., 1918-1988. 2. World War, 1939-1945—Medical care—United States. 3. Queen Mary (Steamship) 4. World War, 1939-1945—Personal narratives, American. 5. Medical personnel—United States—Biography. 6. United States. Army—Biography.
I. Justak, Martine H. II. Title.
D807.U74Q453 1989   89-83493
940.54'7573—dc20   CIP

ISBN 0-9622964-0-6 (pbk)
Library of Congress Catalog No.89-83493

PRINTED IN THE UNITED STATES OF AMERICA

This book is affectionately dedicated

To Seelig O. Freund, M.D., Lt. Col., U.S.A. Medical Corps (Ret.), whose professional competence, integrity, and dedication were unique, whose human compassion was unlimited, and whose example of what a man can be inspired my life.

To Leigh Travers Smith (died, 1946, aged thirty-six hours), whose death changed everything for me.

To Leigh Marie Copeland (12/31/70–1/13/85) our adopted daughter, who, being afflicted with cystic fibrosis, taught us how to risk each hour joyfully in the shadow of death.

Robert R. Copeland

A note from the editor . . .

One day several summers ago Bob and Barbara Copeland came to see me about some business matters, and in the course of what turned out to be a delightful afternoon of conversation on the terrace, Bob happened to remark that he had written a book some years before relating his experiences during World War II as a medic on the *Queen Mary*. I told him I would like very much to read the manuscript, and that was all it took—the next day he dumped a large box full of 8-1/2 × 11 paper on my doorstep.

I was fascinated by the story he had to tell, another footnote, I thought, to the history of World War II, which was, after all, my very own war. So I offered to edit the manuscript for him, provided I could do it at my leisure.

Bob was agreeable to my self-serving terms, and that was the beginning of our collaboration, which continued over the next year during which I had, regrettably, very little "leisure." I guess I would have been less dilatory had I known what a sick man he was. Bob had a heart murmur left over from his bouts with rheumatic fever as a child, and during that year of 1988, when I was working on the manuscript in fits and starts, he began to suspect that his dramatic loss of weight was due to a heart problem; and when he finally went to see a doctor he was advised he would need a valve replacement immediately.

Bob had the operation in October, 1988. It was apparently successful, and he was full of hope for the future. His dearest wish, I think, was to organize a reunion of the men who were permanent staff of the U.S. Army Hospital on the *Queen Mary* during World War II, and to hold the reunion in Long Beach, California, where they could walk the decks of their ship together again.

By the end of November I had, finally, finished the major editing of the manuscript and gave it to him to go over, to make any corrections he thought necessary. He finished reading the revised manuscript and writing out his suggestions on a Tuesday, and the next day suffered a massive stroke which resulted in his death December 3, 1988. I know he was satisfied with the way the book turned out. I also know it might have been much better had he lived.

There are still a number of men and women out there who lived through World War II, who will read Bob's book and suddenly be projected backward in time to a simpler, more straightforward era in our history. For these people it will bring back a flood of memories that they have lost touch with—at least that is what one reader told me. For younger people it may provide a human dimension to the cold recitation of facts in their history books. If you enjoy it, please write to tell us, care of the publisher. There are several other people who contributed to bringing this book into print:

... my good friend, Alice Berman Roth, of Indianapolis, Indiana, who went over the manuscript with the professional writer's attention to minor details.

... my telephone acquaintance, Bill Roush, of Pioneer, California, described by Bob Copeland as the "best damn sergeant in the U.S. Army." Bill was able to verify some facts that I needed to check, and finally, after a good bit of arm-twisting, sent me the picture of himself as a young non-com that we have reproduced.

... another telephone acquaintance, Bill Winberg, of the *Queen Mary* archive department, who read the manuscript, and has been generous with assistance and advice, as well as providing many of the photographs included in the book, and documentation that enabled me to correct minor errors in Bob's memory of the timing of events.

... my friend, Barbara Copeland, who has been an enthusiastic collaborator, first with Bob, and later with me.

... and, of course, my very best friend, Ray Justak, who makes everything possible.

Martine H. Justak
May, 1989

Table of Contents

Foreword

I had the opportunity of working with Robert Copeland in 1981 when he first began gathering his notes and recollections for *Warrior Without Weapons*. Bob made several nostalgia-filled trips to the *Queen Mary* for advice, inspiration and historical information about the period he served aboard the ship. I was able to hear many of his accounts personally, and fortunately for us, Bob wrote as he talked, in a midwest style with a knack for storytelling second to none. And what stories he had to tell!

Warrior Without Weapons acquaints us with many of the personalities that the *Queen Mary* transported during World War II—the staff of the ship's hospital, wounded heroes, statesmen, prisoners of war, war brides—even a newborn baby whose life Bob worked hard to save. It is also the story of the ship he loved: the *Queen Mary*.

She was officially classified as *His Majesty's Transport*, but more commonly known as "The Gray Ghost," for her great speed and ability to slip in and out of faraway harbors. It was said that the capability of the *Queen Mary* and her sister ship, the *Queen Elizabeth*, to ferry up to 15,000 soldiers at a time to any area shortened World War II by a full year.

I am happy that I had the opportunity of participating in the development of this book, and proud to say that I had the chance to know Bob Copeland personally. He was one of the thousands of unsung heroes of World War II who did their jobs, often in impossible situations and under unbearable conditions, but who always have a story to tell. This is Bob's story.

William M. Winberg
Exhibits/Archives Supervisor
R.M.S. Queen Mary
Long Beach, California
May, 1989

Chapter 1

IN THE BEGINNING

How we met

There she was—the most beautiful ship ever to sail the seas, and I remember the awe I felt when I first saw her nestled up to Pier 90 in New York. She was painted battleship gray, to camouflage her purpose, but the drab color couldn't hide the fluidity of her lines, and even from my distant vantage point she dominated the harbor and made the other ships seem insignificant by comparison.

I wasn't there when the *Queen Mary* first relinquished her civilian garb and became *His Majesty's Transport Queen Mary*; and the pride of the Cunard line had been carrying troops for several years before I first saw her in January of 1945. But from that moment until the day sixteen months later when I ceased being Sergeant Copeland and became plain Mr. Copeland again, I had a love affair with *HMT Queen Mary*, and probably spent as much time with her, listening to the heartbeat of her engines and catering to the needs of her subjects, as any other American. Perhaps more time than any Britishers, too, except for some of the merchant crew who had been with her when she was a passenger liner, and who stayed with her during World War II.

And from that hour when we first met until we parted, I
made nineteen crossings of the Atlantic with the First Lady of
the Seas, and logged 130,000 miles on her decks. And then our
paths diverged, and she went her way and I went mine. I didn't
see her again for forty years, when my beauty had become ob-
solete and too expensive to maintain: in 1967 she was sold to
promoters and drydocked in Long Beach, California. She had
become a tourist attraction for vacationing families from all
over the world.

When I visited her, and walked the decks again that had
been my home in 1945 and 1946, I bought one of the pamphlets
that related some of her history during those years, and memories flooded back, in living color. I began recalling events in
which I had been a participant, anecdotes that would flesh out
the dry recitation in the pamphlet that she had "served as a
troop transport during World War II," and had carried
wounded and war brides. So I sat down to write a paragraph or
two about some of the incidents that I still remembered as vividly as though they had happened yesterday, and found my
life was so intertwined with hers during that period that I had
to relate a few events in which I was an actor that did not directly involve the *Queen*. But it seemed necessary to include
them to give something of the special flavor of those years.

Personal history

I guess I should tell you a little about myself first. I was born
June 18, 1918 on a small farm near Cross Plains, Indiana,
which is down near the Ohio River. I was the eldest of the
seven children of Earl Joseph and Grace Porter Copeland, two
hard-working people of Irish and Scottish descent.

After I finished high school my parents thought I deserved a
vacation before settling down to help Dad on the farm, and
they sent me to visit relatives in Indianapolis for a few days.
The few days turned out to be the rest of my life—because
while I was there I learned that Holliday Steel Mill had some

job openings, so I lied about my age (I was seventeen), and was hired. After a couple of years I found a better-paying job at the street car company, first as a motorman and then as a supervisor. And I never did get back to the farm to live.

Two events occurred when I was nineteen that were to control the future course of my life: I married Margaret, my high school sweetheart; and the war in Europe began. By the time I was twenty-three the United States had gotten into the fracas, and Margaret and I had one son and a modest five-room house that was almost paid for.

The outlook was gloomy for the Allies in those early years, and I wanted desperately to get into the fight. But the streetcar company had listed my job as "essential," and I was never called. In 1942 Margaret gave birth to another son, which made me feel even more of a shirker. I thought a man with a family had a lot more reason to fight for his country than most of the eighteen and nineteen year-old boys who were being called up.

Finally, in early 1944 (against my father's advice: "One person can't make a difference, Bob") I overrode the transit company's objections, volunteered for the Army, and was inducted and sent to Camp Barkeley in Abilene, Texas, for the standard six weeks' basic training.

I had requested the infantry. But the Army in its infinite wisdom sometimes overrules soldier's preferences, and it had no hesitation in overruling mine. I was shipped to the Medical Technician's School at Fort Sam Houston, Texas. That was like being in heaven after sweltering through the hottest months of the decade in Abilene. In the summer of 1944 any place in Texas where there was a water cooler was heaven, and at Fort Sam Houston we did at least have a water cooler.

I only had a few weeks at the technician's school. Medics were greatly in demand and short in supply, so the Army brass figured on-the-job training would be just as valuable as book work. Some of us were assigned to the surgery at Brooke General Hospital in San Antonio, and because it looked as if we might stay there for awhile, Margaret and the boys came down to Texas to live, which was wonderful even though I didn't get off the base to see them very often.

The officers at Brooke organized us into medical units. The medics were being prepared, they said, to be part of close-knit, highly skilled mobile teams of surgeons and medics who would follow behind the first wave of the invasion of Europe and set up front-line surgeries to take care of the wounded, who might otherwise die before they could be evacuated. It sounded like a brilliant concept to me.

Casualties were already being shipped back from Africa and the Pacific. For ninety days we lived and breathed surgery. Trainloads of wounded arrived at Brooke, and there was no rest for any member of the staff until every soldier on a train had been treated. Sometimes it took almost seventy-two hours to clear out all the patients, and for the medics, working without respite several times around the clock, benzedrine had to take over to supply the energy that sleep would otherwise have provided.

Under the supervision of Captain Rose Macias, in civilian life a head nurse at Charity Hospital in New Orleans, we nine medics not only worked the wards, but also "scrubbed" and assisted surgeons, so we got a pretty thorough grounding in current medical techniques and emergency procedures.

In addition, because I needed to earn more money than the Army saw fit to pay me, I got a weekend job at Bexar County Hospital in San Antonio as assistant to the intern in charge of the emergency room. I said "in charge," but in reality he *was* the emergency room staff until I got there on Saturday nights. After the intern, whose name I have long since forgotten, found out I knew how to thread a needle, I did a lot of suturing, because there was a lot of suturing to do. San Antonio on Saturday nights in 1944 was a kind of battlefield of its own: we got the victims of gun fights and domestic arguments and alcoholic fracases. Snakebites and ptomaine poisoning were routine.

Between Brooke General and Bexar County I couldn't have had a better education for a medic.

Sadistic sergeant

One thing happened during my tenure at Brooke that people may find unbelievable and I am reluctant to relate it, but it did happen, and it should be told.

I was young and naive and idealistic and patriotic, in short the average American soldier of World War II. We had a clear sense of purpose then, all of us: we knew that Hitler had to be fought to the death if the free world was to survive; we knew about the atrocities committed by the Nazis; and we knew that our people were more civilized than the Germans, and would never commit or tolerate deliberate cruelty towards man or race as they had done.

Therefore, when I heard scuttlebutt around the hospital about a non-com who was abusing patients, I didn't give it any credence. Rumors in hospitals can get around very fast and be blown up out of all proportion.

But one day—it was November 17, 1944, to be exact—about 9:00 o'clock in the morning I was working in a ward where we had about 100 wounded men in beds lining the walls. I had a privacy curtain pulled shut around a bed while I shaved an Air Force mechanic who had suffered a broken back while working on the wing of a B-17 bomber. We were talking quietly when I heard a young Texan across the aisle pleading, "Sergeant, for God's sake, don't...don't. Oh, please don't..." Pleading, begging, sobbing.

The patient's last name was Lara. He was nineteen years old, and a machine gun had nearly cut him in half at the pelvis. He was in excruciating pain all of the time, and to make it a little more bearable, the doctors had him suspended inside what we called a drum bed—a hollow cylinder with suspension devices inside and a ratchet outside capable of turning the patient in the drum without undue stress on his wounds.

"Sweat, you goddam, miserable, gold-brickin' spic," the sergeant said softly, and I could hear him bump the side of the drum bed with the heel of his hand.

Suddenly, I *knew* what was going on. I knew the rumors I had heard, but discounted, were true, and that this was the non-com the patients in the wards had been complaining about. My reaction was instinctive and immediate and without thought-taking. I could feel my insides twisting with pain, as if I were inside that drum: all of my senses were on alert; all my energies were focussed, and I was consumed by the white fire of rage.

At that time I was six-foot-one and weighed 240 pounds. I had lived on a farm most of my life, doing a man's work since I was nine. I had, moreover, just spent six weeks in basic training camp which is a grueling physical fitness course in any man's language. As a consequence, I was probably capable of exerting more physical strength at that one moment than at any other time in my life, before or since.

The privacy curtains were between me and the sergeant. I don't remember tearing the curtain holders out of the masonry of the side wall in my hurry to get at him. I remember only grabbing the sergeant's arm away from the ratchet with my left hand before my right fist connected with his face. The sergeant may have been a strong man, but he was not a big man, and I had the advantage of surprise. I also had the strength of outrage. I smashed at his face and head and whatever I could find to hit with my fists, and then picked him up with my hands at his neck and his groin and began swinging his body around aloft, probably with the intention of throwing him down and bashing his brains out on the terrazzo floor of the ward.

The men were now shouting, "Kill him, kill him, the dirty bastard." The sergeant's face was a bloody mess, and six teeth had been knocked out of his mouth. Some of the patients who were ambulatory had left their beds, and were standing in the aisle to egg me on. One's senses are unusually acute in such situations, and I remember seeing two men who had each lost a leg in battle struggle to get out of their beds which were next to each other and stand up beside them, each on his one good leg, so they could get a better view.

For some reason, perhaps because I am not by nature a violent man, perhaps because the good Lord was protecting me from my own foolishness, I stopped, and instead of dashing the man down against the floor I dragged him by one leg up and down the aisle in front of the men he had been abusing. Finally, my anger partially assuaged, I let go of him, and watched as he stood up, eyed me cautiously, and backed away from me two or three steps. Then he about-faced quickly and ran out of the ward.

I talked the men into returning to their beds, and quietly continued to shave the soldier with the busted back.

Within ten minutes a Military Police lieutenant and two MP tech sergeants entered the ward, all three carrying Thompson machine guns, and one of the sergeants a set of chains slung over his shoulder. I stepped out into the aisle of the ward, and tried to reassure them. Obviously someone had told them one of the medic trainees had gone off his rocker, and they were taking no chances.

"You don't have anything to fear from me," I said.

"That's not what we heard," the lieutenant said, "You're under arrest," and he set the end of the barrel of his Tommy gun against my nose while one of the sergeants used the chains to shackle my hands and feet.

In this fashion, with the lieutenant walking in front and the two sergeants, their machine guns poking into my backside, in the rear, we proceeded through the hospital, down the elevator to the main floor, and out across the compound to detachment headquarters. With my feet manacled I could only take little, mincing steps, and we had to walk about three quarters of a mile, so it took some time to get to the office of our commanding officer, Major J.S. Pickel.

I knew enough about Army regulations concerning the penalty for attacking a superior in rank to know I was in for real trouble. I was looking at a future which would probably include spending the next fourteen years of my life in an Army prison.

Major Pickel, who had charge of all the enlisted personnel at Brooke, was a stern man, a Texan, and a tough hombre in his own right. He didn't look down at his desk when he talked to you—he looked straight at you, like his eyes were the business end of two 45-caliber pistols. The major was not a man to be trifled with. This was the first time I had come face to face with him.

Major Pickel looked at me, and at the chains and the three Tommy guns.

"Release this man, Lieutenant," he said, "I'll take full responsibility. And you can go about your duties."

He motioned for the lieutenant to leave and for the two sergeants to move to the side of the room.

Then Major Pickel picked up a pamphlet and read aloud the Articles of War which I had violated and asked me if I understood them, and understood that a general court martial would be convened to conduct my trial, and I said I did.

"Now, then, Private Copeland, do you have anything to say?"

Those gun barrel eyes were piercing into me, but I compelled myself to look straight back at him. I was in for it, and I was scared, but I didn't intend to grovel.

"Yes, sir, Major Pickel, I have a request and I have a statement."

My request was that he personally investigate the matter and not delegate the task to anyone else; and then I told him my version of what had happened, and concluded by saying that as far as I was concerned, the sergeant's conduct was a disgrace to our country, to the Army, and to the Army Medical Corps; but most of all, I said, it was a disgrace to him because the sergeant was one of his men.

Then I looked him straight in the face.

"Major," I said, "if I spend one day in an Army prison because of this, I serve notice here and now your court martial will be passing a death sentence on this sergeant. Because when I finish my sentence I will hunt him down, and when I find him I will kill him as I almost did, and probably should have done, today."

The major cleared his throat and peremptorily dismissed the two MPs who had remained in the room.

"Sounds like you mean that."

"Yes, sir, I do."

The major looked down at the manual in front of him. He appeared to be considering various options.

Finally, he said, "I'm going to respect your request and will investigate the matter personally. But in the meantime you are under arrest. Unfortunately, this is war, medics are in short supply, and we need your services. Therefore, pending a court martial you will continue your training and your work while under arrest. You will have a triangle to operate in: your bed, your work assignment, and the mess hall. Get out of that triangle and you will be jailed from the end of your work day until the next work day. Master Sergeant Srubar will meet you each morning to give you your assignment. Is that all clear?"

I nodded.

"You're dismissed, then. And for God's sake, go take care of that hand. It's bleeding."

The arrest, of course, put an end to my extra tour of duty at Bexar County Hospital, and I wasn't able to leave the base to see my wife and sons, but aside from those minor limitations no army private or trainee facing a court martial was ever treated as considerately as I was.

Have you heard the term "guard house lawyer?" They were everywhere, offering advice. Mostly they would say, "They can't do this to you; you've got a right to a speedy trial; demand a court martial; demand a pardon."

The guys meant well, but the last thing I wanted was a trial. I felt that right was on my side, and I stayed calm, or at least I tried to. The only thing I couldn't bring myself to do was tell my wife that there was a possibility I was going to jail for fourteen years. Instead, I kept assuring her that my continued absence from our San Antonio apartment was because of the never-ending flood of wounded we had to care for. Which was not a total lie, anyway.

Then one day I was assisting Major Robertson, a fine brain surgeon, during an operation, when someone on the other side of the
table pointed to the outer door. There, looking through the glass
and motioning for me to come out, was Sergeant McGinnis from
Major Pickel's office. I shook my head. Surely he knew we
couldn't just leave surgery at any time. Finally, we closed the flaps
of skin over the scalp and bandaged the patient's head, and I was
able to meet Sergeant McGinnis in the hallway.

"Copeland," he said, "let's go down to the latrine. I have a
message for you."

What a place, I thought, to learn the date for the trial which
is going to send you to prison for the best years of your life.

I'll never know why the sergeant chose the latrine to deliver
his message.

"Copeland," he said, when we were safely behind the doors
of the men's restroom, "the Major was called away today, but
before he left he gave me a message for you. First, he said to tell
you he has investigated the charges personally, as you requested, and finds your version of what happened entirely correct. Second, he said to give you this ten spot, to tell you that it
comes out of his own army pay, and he's damn proud to have a
man like you in his command"—here McGinnis drew a $10 bill
out of his pocket and handed it to me—"and only regrets God
didn't put him in your shoes that morning. And finally he said
to tell you that you're free of arrest and all restrictions. Your
record has been cleared, and all mention of your action against
the sergeant expunged."

What happened to the sadistic sergeant? As soon as his injuries healed he was transferred to Infantry Replacement at
Camp Fannin, Tyler, Texas, and that was the last I ever heard
of him.

First crossing

As I said, there were nine of us in that group of trainee medics. The Army had since found out by hard experience that

Training at Camp Barkeley, Texas, 1944. Voted "most popular spot in America to be bombed."

Medic group at Brooke General Hospital, Fort Sam Houston, Texas. Author standing, left.

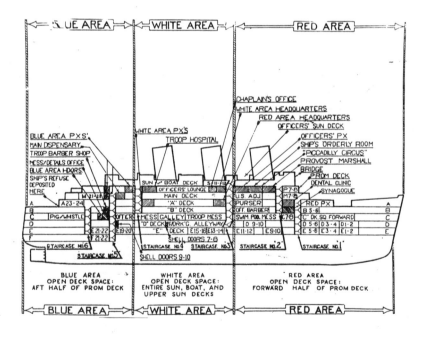

This was the "red, white and blue sheet" given troops boarding the Queen to help them find their way around the ship.

there was no way beach hospitals could function under fire. The idea, which had seemed so novel in the early years of the war, was shelved, and the nine of us were sent to different postings. My destination was Fort Hamilton, in Brooklyn, New York, and after that, there were what seemed endless days of waiting until orders came through. But finally come through they did, and the rumor that several of us were to staff the Army Hospital on the *Queen Mary* proved true. And there I was at the gangplank, gawking up at Her Highness.

Any ritual of the changing of the staff in those days while the war was raging furiously in both major theaters, was a myth. The etiquette of peacetime transfer was submerged in wartime necessity. Without fanfare, we boarded an almost empty ship. There were perhaps 150 medics, some of them doctors and other practitioners, but a good twenty per cent medics by Army fiat only, plucked from other jobs in the Military Police or Army post offices to fill a void in the personnel roster. And not all of them were happy about it. We had, in fact, a group of chronic complainers. Some of them made calls before we got underway, to their congressmen, to previous commanding officers—to anyone they thought might have some influence to get them different duty assignments. These fellows never carried their weight as medics, and never ceased to bitch to anyone who would listen. They were particularly offensive on the homeward-bound voyage when we were carrying wounded, men who had something to complain about, but didn't. We called those disaffected medics the "spoiled brats," and tried to keep them out of our hair as much as possible, but in the end they managed to cause their share of trouble.

The *Queen* was like a floating city: there were twelve decks and it took about as much time to learn one's way around her intricate passages as it would to learn the layout of a small town. I was no exception that first day. I made a number of false turns in the process, but finally found my way to D deck, starboard side, and to the room which was to be my sleeping quarters for the next five months. I shared it with fourteen other men. We slept on canvas racks with stanchion supports. I think the theory was that if you worked hard enough and got tired enough you could sleep anywhere. And it proved true.

Even as I was stowing away my duffel bag beneath the bedrack a voice over the loudspeaker advised us in clipped British accents that the troops would begin boarding at 2300, and I knew we had to get organized to handle patients. So by asking directions of every seaman I saw, and retracing my steps a few times I finally found my way up to the hospital, which was aft on the Sun Deck, in the area which had been the Verandah Grill when the *Queen* was a passenger liner.[1] Some of the medical personnel were already there, the ones who had I guess, like me, been blessed with adaptable inner ears and were not already incapacitated by the swaying of the deck beneath them.

Embarkation of troops began, and the loudspeaker constantly bleated out directions, keeping the lines flowing in the right lanes, to the right decks and the assigned quarters. Getting 15,000 troops and gear aboard and sorted out in some sequence with respect to platoon and company requires a bit of logistical expertise, and this the voice over the loudspeaker must have had, because every loading I ever witnessed was accomplished with the least confusion and the greatest dispatch imaginable for such an operation.

But nevertheless, the embarkation process took hours and hours. By dawn it was complete, and the loudspeakers gave instructions for placing the last mail in the red censor box near the main gangplank, always the last item of business before sailing. Some of our staff hustled past the censor box and off the ship with a final letter to a mother, a sweetheart, or a wife, and mailed them where they were not supposed to, in the regular mailboxes out on 12th Avenue, down the street from Pier 90. But I was busy going through supplies in the operating

---

1. Ed. note: Before and after the war the ship's hospital, operating theatre, and dispensary were located in much smaller quarters on C Deck, portside, midship. The medical personnel consisted of two surgeons and a staff of ten. There were accommodations for twenty patients in the main hospital, and for ten in the infectious ward, which was on B deck at the very stern of the ship.

room cabinet. I didn't want to take time to leave the ship, so I put my letter to my wife and sons in the red box. I had led Margaret to believe that we were going on a hospital ship, so I wanted to let her know this wasn't true.

"Contrary to what I thought, the *Queen Mary* is not a hospital ship. She is an armed transport with what I counted as fifty-one guns."

I thought this bit of information would appeal to the boys; and Margaret, now that she was living back home in Indiana with her parents, always wanted to know as much as she could about where I was and what I was doing. I would have liked to tell her more about the embarkation process, which impressed me greatly, but there wasn't time, so it had to be a short letter.

The U.S. Army Station Hospital on the *Q.M.*, had a 250-bed capacity. My first interest was the operating room, of course, but what I saw there was a far cry from the nine well-equipped operating theaters back at Brooke. Most of our equipment was out of date, compared to the state of the art equipment we had at Brooke. I did find, when I went poking around, that at least the instrument cabinet was well-stocked: there were even some obstetrical and gynecological instruments. I had to laugh when I saw them. I hadn't seen any female troops during the embarkation process, but one learns the Army Supply Corps has a logic all its own. We did have a small complement of female nurses and technicians with us that trip, and perhaps this was reason enough for those instruments.

Our immediate commanding officer was a physician from Cleveland, Ohio named Cohn. Colonel Cohn, about fifty years of age then, was, perhaps, the perfect manifestation of the ideal which most of us have of a medical man, the quintessential doctor. He was skilled, organized, compassionate, and pragmatic. I will always remember him with respect and affection.

Mal de mer

It was early January, 1945, bitter winter in the North Atlantic, and the seas were rough. Most of the 15,000 troops got desperately seasick. There were too few beds for the numbers who were truly sick, so we had to be selective in the ones we took into the hospital, but most of the men who were in bad shape and needed attention either didn't know where the hospital was, or were too debilitated to find their way there. So after the first twenty-four hours at sea Colonel Cohn had some of us patrolling the decks and staircases at night before going off duty to find the sickest ones and carry them to the hospital to get warm, and to get some intravenous fluids into their dehydrated bodies. I personally followed this procedure for all the rest of my trips on the *Queen,* regardless of who was in charge, because seasickness always continued to be a major problem for the medical staff.

As a matter of fact, I do not recall any other serious illnesses during that first crossing. We were totally involved with ministering to seasick troops. We were so busy that we didn't have time for the endless hours of standing in mess lines twice a day to get our meals, so most of us quickly adapted to a diet of Hershey bars and K-rations. The portholes were heavily painted over to shut out the lights inside the ship, and to allow us to glide through the seas at night as silently and inconspicuously as possible. Since we medics were always in the hospital or in our hammocks, the nights blended into days and the days into night. I don't remember any time Dr. Cohn or anyone ever told me I was off duty, and I don't think I saw any part of the ship that first crossing except what was visible in the walk between our quarters on D deck and the hospital six decks above.

Clyde River Anchorage

With the zigzagging we did to avoid submarines the trip from New York to our Clyde River anchorage at the little city of Gourock, Scotland, about fifteen miles downriver from Glasgow, took almost six days.[2]

At the point where it flows into the Atlantic, the Clyde River widens out to make room for many ships to anchor without crowding. Seaward from the anchorage, the hills close in, forming a sheltered bay, and this configuration made it possible for the anchorage to be protected by a steel submarine net stretched across the entrance. The steel submarine net was like a huge pair of underwater curtains, anchored solidly at the shore ends, and held in place midsteam by small vessels, which, at the last moment as our ship approached, would move apart with the steel curtains and close the instant our stern had passed through. To my knowledge, this system worked satisfactorily all during the war—I don't believe a submarine ever penetrated the defenses of the Clyde River Anchorage.

When we got inside the harbour and laid anchor, there was a small coal-burning ship, the *Romsey*, which unloaded and reloaded the *Queen* at the rate of 500 troops per trip. This meant that the *Romsey* had to make thirty round trips back and forth from ship to shore to unload the troops we had carried over, and then another thirty round trips to re-load us for the return voyage.

After a few passages I got used to this process, but the first time it happened was an eye-opener to me. Night and day the *Romsey* continued to plough her way through the harbour, to and from the *Queen*.

For the medics, loading and unloading at the Clyde River anchorage presented another problem. After the unloading was completed, and the fresh troops were on Scottish soil, we had to bring 2,250 hospital mattresses up from the cargo hold deep inside the ship. There were several ways of doing this. Some men worked in pairs, one man climbing the vertical steel

---

2. Ed. note: The extent of the zigzagging and course alterations the captains felt to be necessary is evident in the logs of these voyages which record distances as great as 3,750 nautical miles for the westward-bound crossings as compared with a maximum of 3,291 nautical miles from Gourock to New York after the end of the war in Europe; and a maximum of 3,645 miles eastward-bound from New York to Scotland as compared with 3,264 immediately after the cessation of hostilities.

ladders between decks with a mattress strapped to his back by canvass bindings, and the other standing below to push up against the mattress and lighten the load. I usually found it easier to work alone, but either way it was a back-breaking feat of strength to climb straight up the ladders from the cargo hold seven decks below to the Main Deck where we had our expanded hospital quarters. And if it had not been for the endurance tests we had been through at Camp Barkeley in basic training, I might not have been able to talk my body into serving me so well.

These mattresses enlarged our facilities for the return trip from 250 beds, which was generally adequate for the outgoing voyage, to a 2,500 bed capacity which was needed for the return trip when we were loaded with wounded men being shipped back to state-side hospitals. The whole ordeal of transporting these mattresses to and from the holds of the ship was reversed when we unloaded the wounded in New York, and this process was repeated every voyage until August of 1945, by which time most of the wounded had been brought back to the States.

British inefficiency

We appreciated the importance of the small ships whose only function during the war was to open and close the submarine nets, but we wondered whether the British war vessels, usually a battleship, but sometimes an aircraft carrier, which always manned the harbour, were really necessary and could not be put to better use elsewhere. Every trip we made, back and forth across the Atlantic, there they were, sometimes one, usually two of them, rolling gently on the harbour swells, apparently without function. It was dismaying to some of us, who thought the British could deploy their ships more efficiently, and that certainly we Americans should have done so. Then one afternoon our view of their function was abruptly altered. Somehow, while we were anchored in the bay, a Nazi dive bomber managed to penetrate our air space, and came down through the overcast, which was up around 3,000 feet. All at once the harbour exploded skyward as the British warship, the *Formidable*, threw up a triangle of smoking explosives.

A hit was made, and as we watched from the *Queen's* deck, first bombs and engine parts fell from the sky, then shrapnel from the *Formidable's* explosives, then the fuselage of the Nazi plane and the pilot's body, and finally the lightweight body of the fighter plane with its ugly black swastika. Most of the bombs falling from the target plane detonated in the air, but at least one exploded on impact with the Clyde River, and then cheers went up from our decks, and signal blinkers from the quarterdecks of all the other ships in the harbour, saluting the men of the *Formidable*. And never again did I hear anyone on the *Q.M.* complain about the British ship that was malingering out there in the center of the Anchorage.

The return trip

Well, I am getting far ahead of my story. After the *Romsey* got us unloaded that first trip, the medics were permitted eight hours ashore before the re-loading began. Everyone headed for Glasgow, and mostly we just wandered around that city until the deadline for returning to the ship. The hospital trains were already approaching the quay as we travelled shore to ship via the *Romsey*.

We were the first to board, and then came eight or ten trips to load the wounded. That ordeal took a day and a half. It was like the hospital trains of Brooke General all over again. We quickly used up all the beds equipped with the mattresses we had brought up from the hold. So then we had to settle some of the less seriously wounded on canvas racks on stanchions like the ones we slept on ourselves. But I never heard one man complain about the primitive accommodations. These were the

The Verandah Grill before it was converted into the Troop Hospital.

The Queen *anchored at Gourock, Scotland.*

men who had recently been christened in battle; they were just glad to be among the lucky ones to go home.

After all the wounded were loaded, we took aboard about 10,000 ex-combat soldiers and airmen who were being rotated back to the States for reassignment and retraining, either for state-side duty or service in the Pacific theater. This became the typical pattern of our operation until the end of the war. The only variation was a heavier proportion of wounded in ratio to troops after the Battle of the Bulge.

The *Queen* did not sail in convoy like other troop ships. Her speed and size made it difficult for slower ships to convoy her. We were, however, escorted, usually by two or three blimps from Lakehurst, New Jersey, for about 200 miles out of New York; and we were customarily met by a British warship, usually a cruiser, about 200 miles west of Scotland.

Although the *Queen* was equipped with fire power, her real protection from German subs and warships lay in her constant zigzagging; in her speed; and in her radar. Her speed made her a difficult target for the slower-moving subs; her radar gave her an advantage over ships which were not yet so equipped; and the constant zigzagging made it more difficult for the enemy to get a fix on her.

On that first trip over, the constant zigzagging to elude torpedo attack hadn't bothered me, but westbound with all the wounded, the captain intensified his diversionary tactics. The huge ship altered course every five-plus minutes, and one had to develop a kind of inner time clock to adjust his stance on the deck, and to avoid doing injury to the patient he was working with when the ship made its abrupt swing around.

The *Queen* was also armed, which was her principal defense against attack from the air. As I had mentioned in my last letter to my wife before leaving the States I had counted fifty-one guns. I still don't know anything about the types or names of them, or the fire power they represented, but there were two, one at each end of the docking bridge which I came to feel were *my* guns, because I had been designated first aid man to these gun stations.

"BoFors multiple barrel 40MM anti-aircraft cannon" was the legend stamped on them, but the British lovingly referred to them as "Pom-Poms." I surmised that these particular guns had been placed where they were specifically to protect the bridge, and the vital people and instruments contained there, in the event of attack.

At one time there were 225 gunners assigned to man the artillery on the *Queen*; but never in the time I crossed back and forth with her was it ever necessary to fire those guns. We had drills and practice firing—the captain was a stickler for this—but to my knowledge the only casualty we ever had was a gunner who was swept overboard one stormy night when we responded to "battle stations."

However we were always in a state of readiness. On every crossing we passed numerous oil slicks and pieces of wreckage floating on the ocean waves, and they were stark reminders that the seas, even when becalmed, were still fraught with lurking dangers. Also, we knew, or at least we had heard, that Hitler had offered a quarter of a million dollar bounty to any of his submarine captains who was able to hit the *Queen Mary* with a torpedo. The way she was made, one torpedo would not have been able to sink the *Queen*. At the D deck level the ship is divided into sections which, when the watertight doors are closed, will save the ship.

But, nevertheless, any torpedo which hit the *Queen* would have wreaked disaster on a monstrous scale. There's a five letter word which applies here, and it's spelled **P-A-N-I-C**. With 15,000 passengers on board all trying to escape at the same time, jamming the gangways and stampeding the lifeboats, inevitably a great many would have perished in the resulting confusion and melee.[3]

---

3. Ed. note: The lesson of the *Titanic* had been well learned by British ship designers. The *Queen* was equipped with twenty-four diesel-powered lifeboats, each holding 145 persons, for a total capacity of 3,480. This was adequate to take care of any peacetime emergency when she carried a maximum of 1,957 passengers and a crew of 1,174, or a total of 3,131 persons, but would not have been adequate for her normal wartime load of 15,000 troops plus crew.

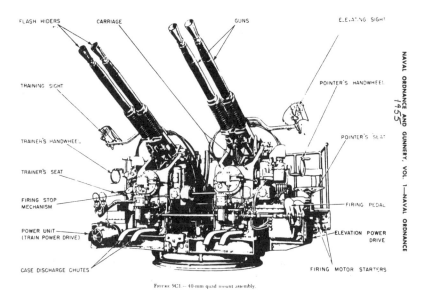

FLASH HIDERS   CARRIAGE   GUNS   ELEATING SIGHT

TRAINING SIGHT

POINTER'S HANDWHEEL

TRAINER'S HANDWHEEL

POINTER'S SEAT

TRAINER'S SEAT

FIRING STOP
MECHANISM

FIRING PEDAL

POWER UNIT
(TRAIN POWER DRIVE)

ELEVATION POWER
DRIVE

CASE DISCHARGE CHUTES

FIRING MOTOR STARTERS

FIGURE 9C1 — 40-mm quad mount assembly.

One of thse gun mountings was on each end of the catwalk to protect
the bridge in case of attack. My first aid post was on the catwalk in
front of the helmsmen.

Manning the guns on the Promenade Deck aft.

Front view of gun emplacements.

Copeland, the Spy

With all the zigzagging the return trip took took even longer than the trip over. Finally we made port and got all the troops ashore and the wounded routed to hospitals at Valley Forge, Fort Dix Station, and Halloran General in New York. We stowed the mattresses back down in the hold, and the medics were ready for shore leave like everybody else.

Except when we lined up on deck, my name was called out, and when I stepped forward I was informed I was under arrest for "giving aid and comfort to the enemy."

The administrative commander of our unit was an officer from Ohio named Captain Perry. I couldn't believe what was happening. Here I had been working my tail off night and day, and I was under arrest. And there were the hell-raisers, the spoiled brats, the original gold bricks, blithely taking off on shore leave.

Captain Perry, with some chagrin, explained what had happened. When the ship docked, he said, some Pentagon officials had come on board in response to all the complaints made by the troublemakers before we left New York. The U.S. Troop Commander, whom I shall, for purposes of his anonymity in case he is still alive, call Colonel Richards, reacted by trying to find a scapegoat, and the only thing he could come up with was my letter to my wife, posted in the red censor box. The censor had kicked it back for containing "secret" information that gave "aid and comfort to the enemy," the infamous material being my recitation in my letter to Margaret that the *Queen Mary* was not a hospital ship, but "a troopship with fifty-one guns."

Some secret! Over 6,000,000 New Yorkers who could count as high as fifty-one shared that secret. But my tail was the one that got caught in the wringer. The brass needed a scapegoat. And I was it.

The upshot was that I was ordered to stay on board ship, and to keep working. The spoiled brats got their transfers, and left for cushy jobs provided by the intervention of their congressmen or their wealthy relatives. But I was like the protagonist in Nathan Hale's *Man Without a Country*, sentenced to stay on shipboard for an indeterminate time, until the powers above saw fit to commute my punishment.

Fortunately, Captain Perry was on my side. My sentence was not lifted until the *Queen* had touched land five times after that. And then it was only because Captain Perry, who had done everything else he could think of to clear my record, without success, finally threatened to resign his commission in protest. That unselfish gesture got someone's attention, and my sentence was lifted. I don't flatter myself that the Army finally acted to correct an injustice to an insignificant private. I think the upper echelons probably valued Captain Perry's services and didn't intend to lose a good officer. They promptly refused Captain Perry's resignation, restored my privileges, and that was the end of that.

Life has its little ironies, however. About 9:00 o'clock one evening, about a week before my detention was lifted, Colonel Cohn came to me in the ward and asked me to go check on Troop Commander Colonel Richards's condition, since he was suffering from a bad cold and bronchitis. I still bore a grudge against the Troop Commander, so I probably didn't respond to the request with much grace. However, when I opened the door to his quarters I could hardly believe my eyes. The room was filled with smoke and one wall was ablaze. Someone hadn't secured the vaporizer properly, and when the ship rolled it had apparently slid over to the bulkhead and set the paper draperies on fire.

I remember having a few murderous thoughts, like, walk around for a few minutes, chum, and let the smoke do the bastard in; but I already had a love affair going with the *Queen*, and I couldn't let a fire get started which might get out of control and damage my Lady. So I pulled the fire alarm, and then crawled along the deck and yanked the burning draperies off the bulkhead and carried them into the bathroom, where I managed to douse the flames. The firemen rushed in just as I was coming out of the bathroom with the soggy remains of the draperies, and then we all quietly tiptoed out together. The whole affair hadn't disturbed the colonel's peaceful slumber. He continued to snore, and if anyone ever told him it was his whipping boy who had saved him from a probable death by fire or suffocation, it certainly wasn't I. And if anyone else ever told him, it certainly never had any effect on his conduct towards me.

Nevertheless, his days as U.S. Troop Commander were numbered. I believe it was on our next return voyage that a New York pilot boat was sent out to the *Queen* as we were leaving the harbor eastbound again. Colonel Richards was summarily removed from the ship and a new commander named Barnett was brought out to replace him. After I got to know Colonel Barnett better I found out what had happened. Apparently, two of the *Queen's* passengers on the homeward voyage were a couple of young Irish beauties, the daughters of an Irish diplomat. Colonel Richards, who was a heavy tippler and fancied himself somewhat of a lady-killer, graciously offered to take the two girls on a tour of the ship. The tour ended up in his cabin where, probably because his judgment was clouded by the alcohol in his system, he terrified the young ladies by what they considered improper sexual advances. They managed to escape from the cabin, and immediately reported the episode. The Army, for once, acted with some degree of dispatch, and Colonel Richards was promptly relieved of his command. Very few men on the ship were ever aware of what had happened, and I never saw any mention of it in a newspaper of the period, so probably the whole affair was discreetly handled in Washington by an apology.

As for me, I was under arrest for a total of seventy-six days, including the Texas affair, but I never missed a day's work, and never lost a night's sleep because of a guilty conscience. And I left the service, somehow, with an unblemished record!

Chapter 2

THE QUEEN'S MEDICS

The staff

I should give you some idea of how greatly the medical staff changed in numbers while I was on the *Queen*.

When I first boarded she carried a complement of about 150 medical personnel, including fifteen army nurses. Colonel Cohn was our Transport Surgeon. I don't recall where the officers' quarters were, but those of us in the lower ranks were housed five decks down on D deck in tourist class staterooms converted to sleep about fifteen men. The roster was thinned out considerably after our first return to New York, when most of the spoiled brats were transferred off the ship and not replaced.

After our second or third trip to Europe, the staff was cut even more, to between twenty and twenty-five men (no women) and this is the number we kept during our busiest period, when we were bringing back as many as 2,500 wounded to New York with every westward crossing. During that time span we were housed in much more comfortable quarters on A deck, four to six men to a room. I lived in A143.

After August of 1945 our permanent staff was cut back again and in order to take care of all the wounded we often had to resort to requesting the help of medical personnel attached to army units returning on the ship. But on my next to last trip, in April, 1946, our staff was increased by fifteen WAC medics.

From the time I got on the ship until around July, 1945, Colonel Cohn was our Transport Surgeon. After he left, Major Seelig Freund of New York City, came aboard. Major Freund joined us in England and served as our Transport Surgeon until February of 1946. For my last eight trips (sixteen crossings) Captain Carl F. Glienke from Wisconsin was Transport Surgeon. The *Queen* only made one more crossing after I left her in New York in April, 1946, and then went into drydock to be refitted for peacetime service. I assume that Captain Glienke made this last trip with her.

Personnel

A141 and A143 housed most of the medics, but who was on the ship at any particular time varied. Anecdotes about some of these people appear later, but here are thumbnail sketches of a few of the men I recall in particular:

In A143

1st Sgt. William Roush, a schoolteacher from California, who had charge of all the medics, made assignments and did all the record-keeping; a fine gentleman.

Pvt. John Bobb, from Dayton, Ohio, who alternated between the *Queen* and the *Vulcania*, another troopship. John, who was about thirty-six at the time he traveled with us, had been an undertaker in civilian life. The Army found that morticians, with their background in anatomy, made wonderful medics. John was the only soldier I knew who wrote at least part of a letter to his wife every day: his letters, if still available, would give a much more accurate daily account of the medic's life on the *Queen* than do my forty-year-old recollections.

Quartermaster Sgt. Al Shriner, was responsible for medical supplies. He was on the *Queen* before I shipped on, and stayed on after I left. Everyone liked Al.

Louis T. Macaronas, a conscientious Greek fellow from Boston, was our pharmacist and ran a tight shop. Macaronas would scour the ship after the troops had debarked and pick up all the clothing and blankets they had left behind. He used his own money to get the stuff cleaned, and then took it to the Greek Relief Headquarters in New York. Mac found this hard on his pocketbook, so he had the idea of trying to sterilize the stuff by washing it in seawater. He found a sufficiently long section of quarter-inch rope and tied a large bundle of blankets and clothes together. Then with the help of some of us in A143 he got the bundle through the porthole and dropped it down into the sea when we were underway. Mac was heartbroken when he went back some hours later. All that remained was a three-foot length of rope with a frayed end. The friction between the rope and the moving ship had lost war-ravaged Greece one bundle of sorely needed supplies.

Al Fortmuller, from the Bronx, who turned out to be a great guy to work with, but started out rank-happy. I recall making a last patient check at 4:00 a.m. one morning before going off duty, and finding Al sitting and drinking coffee with a brigadier general. It would have been all right, except the general had been brought in the day before with a severe coronary and needed complete bed rest; he had talked Al into letting him get up. I got a stretcher and with Al's help put him on it and carried him back to bed. Later that day Major Freund went in and had a heart-to-heart talk with the general. We told Al later that any medic in the hospital outranked any sick officer, no matter what he wore on his shoulders.

Lucius A. Draper, who also went by the name "Al," was a good ol' boy from Anniston, Alabama. Al didn't have any particular qualifications as a medic, but he was willing, he worked hard, and he was always smiling. The patients loved him.

Howard Ehrich, from Chicago. I have used a pseudonym for him for reasons which will be obvious later. He was our first lab technician.

Seymour T. ("Si") Amkraut, from Brooklyn, replaced Howard Ehrich as our lab technician, and did a fine job. He stayed on the *Queen* for her last trip after I left. His family had a feather importing and processing business in Brooklyn.

Jack Sigmond, from Cleveland, another pseudonym. This fellow was a thoroughly likeable chap, but he had some problems. One was a real fear of torpedoes. He had to take sleeping pills to get any rest at night. I had a bunk on an inside wall, and switched with him so he would feel safer. Sigmond was in charge of food service: he spent his time in the galley making sure that the right food went to the right patients. Twice he went berserk. The first time one of the English engineer officers who had to go through the hospital to get to his duty station came rushing down to the ward where I was working to tell me that one of the medics had gone bonkers. I went back to the galley with him, and there was Sigmond with a wild look in his eyes, throwing coffee cups against the bulkhead, where there was already a sizeable mound of broken china. I took away the cups that he had in his hands ready to throw when we walked in, and suggested he was over-worked and needed to rest for a couple of days. I walked him down to the room and gave him a sedative, and after that he toughed it out until V-J Day when he had another blow-up which I describe later.

In A141

Dean Edward Reilly, from Ames, Iowa, a good friend. He had charge of the isolation hospital.

Lamar T. Crask, who was with Special Services, and had a signed photograph ("To Lamar with all my love") of Lena Horne hung over his bunk. One time when we were docked in New York some of the fellows took off for Times Square and saw Crask with his arm in a black sling, a black patch over one eye, and all sorts of medals fastened on his chest, including a purple heart. We never did learn what the masquerade was about, but some of us had our suspicions.

Jonesy. I don't know any other name for him. He replaced Macaronas as our pharmacist after Mac was discharged. He had a shipboard romance going with one of the WACs. I remember one day when I either wanted something from the pharmacy or was looking for his girlfriend who was supposed to be on duty and found them sacked out in her cabin, both high on drugs cabbaged from the pharmacy.

Herman Ephraim Cohen, another pseudonym. Hermie didn't live with us, but he was a Special Services man attached to the *Queen*, and I will have a bit to say about him later. His name has been changed, not because I want to avoid embarrassing him or his family, but because it is possible, even now, that his cover should not be blown. In any case I once gave my word, and I am still honoring it.

Sick call

Every morning on the *Queen* we had sick call in four or five locations spaced about the ship; and sometimes, because of our limited complement of doctors and medics, these temporary medical sites had to be staffed by transient medical officers attached to units heading for Europe, or coming back from the front, who were routinely generous about donating their time and abilities.

Some of us would try to brief our "temporaries" on the most frequent complaint, which was foreign bodies in the eye. We had developed a sure-fire technique for correcting ninety-nine per cent of these cases, which were caused by ash from the ship's funnels. A little flake would enter the eye, stick to the eyeball, and become totally invisible to scanning with an ophthalmic light. The volunteer doctors almost always would depend on the light instead of our proven method of using a small cotton swab dipped in boric acid solution. So when the doctors would assure the G.I. that whatever it was that had irritated the eye was already gone, if one of the *Queen's* medics was around he would quietly tell the patient—out of earshot of the doctor, of course—to come back at 2:00 p.m., and on that second visit we'd remove the little flake of ash that felt like a large piece of gravel and the patient would go away happy.

Loading wounded troops, Gourock, Scotland.

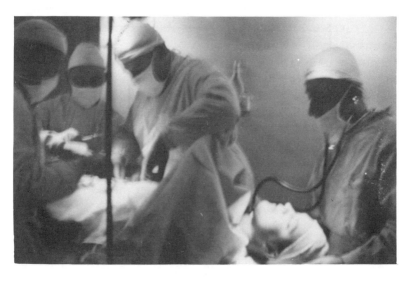

In the Troop Hospital operating room. On the far side of the table (left to right) *John Bobb, the author, Louis Macaronas.*

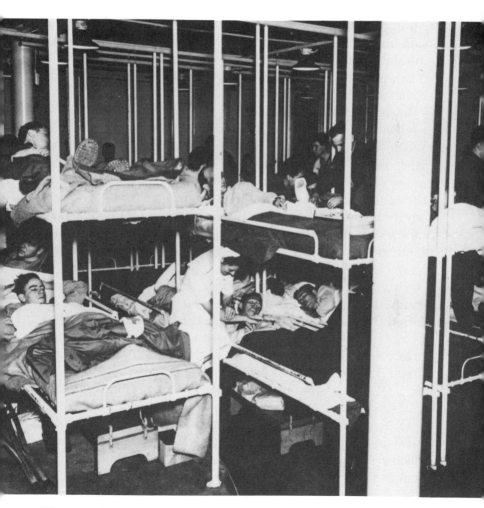

The troop hospital — our most deluxe accommodations.

The other most common problem we faced was scabies, and if you think war is not hell, then you were never infested with scabies.

For the uninitiated, scabies is a contagious skin disease caused by a parasitic mite that burrows under the epidermis of the host to deposit its eggs and propagate its species. The burrowing and the emergence of the progeny to the surface of the skin both cause intense, almost unbearable, itching. The mite inhabits places such as soiled bedding and clothing, and human bodies. The favored area of the human anatomy seems to be around the mid-section, under the belt area.

In those days about the only thing that worked in the battle against scabies was a fairly new chemical discovery, DDT. When our group of medics took over the 200-bed Army Station Hospital on the *Queen* the only assistance we got from the group of medics who had preceded us was a handwritten note thumbtacked to the door of the broom closet from "Kilroy," who not only assured us that he had been there, but allowed as how he had encountered the scabies mite on the ship and lost them in that very spot. He then went on to warn us of the perils of "DDT Rapture."

To kill the mite it was necessary to put the soldier into a compartment as airtight as possible, so that the DDT mist effected the maximum penetration of the pores of the skin. The broom closet was our most airtight enclosure in the hospital area. So our usual procedure was to shut the suffering (and naked) GI in the broom closet which we then sprayed liberally with DDT. It seemed to work and to kill the eggs and emerging mites as well as their parents—we weren't sure quite how.

Of course we didn't know anything about the side-effects of DDT in those days (and probably would not have considered them very important if we had, weighed in the balance against that awful itching), so we used the broom-closet technique routinely. But one day I happened to be in the hospital when a poor scabies victim was pulled out of the closet almost unconscious, a victim of "DDT rapture." I don't know what particular "raptures" were involved, but the end effect of the treatment, if continued over too extended a period, was to knock out the patient. In this soldier's case I was really alarmed, concerned about what could have happened if he had been left in there a few minutes longer.

It was not a cheerful thought. But suddenly, always the improvisor, I remembered the gas mask I had been lugging around in the bottom of my duffel bag since my Camp Barkeley days. Why not? If it was a matter of inhaling the DDT, then why not use a gas mask to allow the soldiers to breathe while they were taking the broom closet treatment? And so it was that my GI issue gas mask became the device for administering DDT to thousands of scabies sufferers from then on. But sure enough, when I was getting mustered-out at Camp Atterbury in Indiana much later, don't you know the Army tried to charge me for a missing item of Army equipment, to wit, one gas mask? But because I had become so used to the ways of the military by that time I immediately expressed an urgent need to find a bathroom, and on the way liberated a gas mask from a pile that I had observed between the counter and the latrine. The harassed supply soldier back at the check-out counter had already forgotten my face and accepted my newly-acquired property as government issue to one Sergeant Robert R. Copeland.

Penicillin

The fatality list of World War II would have been much higher if we hadn't had the benefit of two new "miracle" drugs, sulfa and penicillin. I didn't know anything about the development of sulfa, but I had read about the man who discovered penicillin, the English bacteriologist and Nobel prize-winner, Sir Alexander Fleming. Therefore, I was terribly excited one afternoon when a pleasant-looking middle-aged man in civilian clothes appeared at the door of the operating room and identified himself as Alexander Fleming. It was one of those rare times when I wasn't covered with work, so I gave Sir Alexander a tour of the hospital, and then he just stayed around a couple of hours while we tended to our routine tasks.

To my very great surprise Dr. Fleming told me he had never actually seen a patient being injected with penicillin, and just then, fate being ever-obliging, three young soldiers who had enjoyed one last fling before going overseas, and had loved well, but not wisely, came into the hospital ante-room after getting positive lab tests.

I addressed them as a group:

"Fellas, this gentleman standing next to me is Sir Alexander Fleming of England. Dr. Fleming discovered the germ-killing substance which I have in these syringes; and you have the honor of being the first patients he has ever seen having this drug administered to them. Please drop your trousers—you won't feel a thing."

The GIs were not impressed by my histrionics; one of them said "Hi" to Dr. Fleming, and the others just turned their backsides without acknowledging him at all. After I gave them instructions for further treatment and they went on their respective ways, I tried to apologize to Dr. Fleming for the indifference and lack of respect exhibited by my countrymen.

But Dr. Fleming was not a man imbued with his own self-importance.

"Not to worry," he said, "one cawn't win them all, you know."

"It's Wednesday—it must be gonorrhea"

Most of the doctors and medics on the *Queen* were dedicated, compassionate human beings. We did, however, have our goldbricks, as I have mentioned before, and we did have one laboratory technician who became a real problem for us.

To protect everyone involved, I have given him the pseudonym of "Howard Ehrich."

This young man made a career of taking the easy way out. I can close my eyes now and hear John Bobb or Al Draper raising a ruckus about his leaving his soiled clothing in our living quarters, wherever he shucked it, and deploring the condition of the bathroom after his infrequent trips to the shower. Well, somehow Ehrich had made a friend of an instructor at the technician school, and this instructor saw to it that he made excellent marks and graduated with a high rating; and Howard must have had a good press agent also, because word around the hospital was that Ehrich, despite his slovenly personal habits, was something of an intellectual giant.

I suppose I injected more gallons of penicillin into more soldiers' posteriors than any other needleman in World War II. And on my fourth trip with Ehrich as our lab technician this continued to be true, except for some reason I began to wonder about what looked like a peculiar pattern of infection. One day I'd be busy injecting young men; the next day I wouldn't have any customers at all. The more I thought about it, the more concerned I became. I went to Major Freund and told him about this strange pattern: and he came to the same conclusion that was beginning to haunt me. Our lab man simply didn't know what bacilli looked like! He had been giving us wholly inaccurate reports, and I had been giving 100,000 units of precious penicillin to men who only imagined they had gonorrhea, and, conversely, had been sending some positive cases of venereal disease away, assuring the men that they were not infected.

Since we were still a few hundred miles out from shore at the time we came to this conclusion, we quickly located those we had turned loose, and either Major Freund or I took a look through the microscope ourselves. We were able to correct the mistakes we had made on that crossing, but there were three debarkation groups out there somewhere with soldiers in either one of two categories: (1) men treated with a powerful antibiotic they hadn't needed, which didn't worry us too much; and (2) men with a socially unacceptable disease which they would have no concern about transmitting because I personally had assured them that they were free of disease.

Major Freund did his best: he tried to communicate with shore officials, and get them to put out bulletins on the subject; but we had the depressing feeling we had probably, quite unwittingly, carried an epidemic to Europe and back home again. And it was not a mistake we could rectify.

Needless to say, Lab Technician Ehrich was quickly relieved of duty on the *Queen*, and appropriate remarks inserted into his military record. And that's how the Gray Ghost became home, quite suddenly, to Seymour T. Amkraut, of Brooklyn, New York, a laboratory technician *par excellence*, and one who never had to use the "eenie-meeny-meiny-mo" test to determine who needed my needlework.

War of the *Queen's* medics

Shortly thereafter, and probably because of that episode, someone in the hierarchy of the Army Medical Corps must have decided there needed to be a review of the quality of the medical service we were rendering aboard the *Queen Mary*. God knows, we had been embarrassed by the "fake lab man" fiasco. Major Freund did everything in his power to correct the mistakes that had been made, and there was certainly no attempt to cover up or avoid taking responsibility for the unfortunate results. If anyone was to blame, other than Ehrich and the instructor who had certified him as competent, it was I. I should have been more alert and realized what was happening and exposed Ehrich sooner.

But I guess there had to be some sort of Army investigation to satisfy the brass. So what we got was "Fireball Rose" (as we referred to her among ourselves) and her trio of investigative nurses, to monitor us and all our works.

I didn't know anything unusual was going on: I especially didn't know that we had been assigned a group of Avenging Ladies to peer over our shoulders. So I was totally unprepared for what happened to me next.

We had begun to gain speed off the New Jersey coast, a northeaster was blowing in across our course, and I was getting things secured against the rolling and pitching we could expect from the Atlantic that night. Always, my first routine as we went out to sea was to secure the most expensive piece of surgical apparatus we had, the GOE machine. "GOE" stands for Gas-Oxygen-Ether. In simplest terms, it was the machine that kept a patient furnished with life-sustaining oxygen, combined with the proper mixture of anesthetic gases to maintain the desired level of unconsciousness while he was undergoing surgery. Every Army operating room I ever saw, or worked in, had one. They cost the taxpayers a lot of money, even then, and we treated those machines with a great deal of affection and respect.

I was busy lashing our GOE machine to the sturdy bolted-in-place legs of the operating table when a rather mocking voice called out to me from the open doors of the surgery:

"And what do we have here? A wild west rodeo, perhaps?"

"Fireball Rose" had let loose her first salvo in what was to be a concentrated, but short, little war.

I didn't know her function then, but she was an officer and outranked me, so as patiently as possible I explained to her how a ship rolled and pitched, just as it was beginning to do even then, as the winds of the northeaster began to bite in.

"And, of course, sergeant, that's just why the inventors put those brakes on the wheels!" she said archly, as if I had never noticed them before she brought them to my attention.

I tried to explain, then, that the GOE machine had not been intended for the operating room of a rolling and pitching ship, but for the stable environment of a land hospital. Sure, the brakes worked at Fitzsimmons, at Brooke, and at Camp Shanks Station Hospital; but top-heavy as the equipment was, the brakes did nothing but resist momentum when the Atlantic began to run wild, as it was now beginning to do.

"All right then, sergeant, let me ask you, if tonight at midnight a patient has to have emergency surgery, what will you do then, with all those ropes tied to it?" She was toying with me now, ready for the kill.

"Lieutenant, I would run into this room, pull out this pocket knife, and I'd cut rope like hell!"

It didn't work. Fireball Rose ordered me to cut the ropes pronto and make certain the brakes were set. Then she swept around the room ordering the scrapping of all the other security measures we had come to know, the hard way, were necessary at this particular Army Station Hospital.

No emergency surgery was needed that night, but our night medic, Albert Fortmuller, had a wild few hours. First, the GOE machine did override the brakes and did run amuck inside the operating room, careening wildly around from one wall to the opposite wall until it finally overturned and crashed into the wide double doors of the entrance. The doors were torn off their hinges, and the once-valuable machine lay against the bulkhead opposite in a hopeless mass of rubber bellows, wheels, tubing, glass and chrome.

What turned out to be almost our entire supply of thermometers was gone because I had removed the tape restraints under orders from Fireball. Vital medicines, including dyes, suffered the same fate, and stained what had, until then, been a beautiful parquet floor.

Major Freund, with admirable restraint, kept his temper and ordered the clean-up, but our beloved Fireball Rose and her three nurses didn't show up to help until most of the dirty work was done. We rescued and sorted what materials we had left. The Major and I and our pharmacist, Louis T. Macaronas, had a little test run-through of the procedures involved in the manual administration of oxygen and ether, if surgery became necessary. We thought, if we were not hit by a major catastrophe, we could manage without the GOE: Macaronas could handle the anesthesia and I could administer the oxygen. Major Freund didn't seem to think Fireball or any of her girls would be much help in that event.

But Fireball was not to be denied her triple roles of Teacher, Judge and Executioner. In the course of the next two days at sea, every time the hospital filled with patients, Fireball would call the medics into training classes, leaving the patients virtually unattended. We were "taught" how to read thermometers, take blood pressures and bandage wounds. We were tested on our knowledge of the names and uses of various instruments.

At our last "study hall" one of Fireball's assistants brought forth a rectal tube and smiling sweetly, asked, "All right, who can name this device, and tell me what it is used for?"

There was complete silence from the small group of highly-insulted male medics.

"OK, Private Draper, can you answer my question?" she persisted.

By this time even our genial and courteous southerner had had it.

"Well, lady" (this was Al's first shot in the war; Army nurses were sensitive about being referred to as "ladies"), "I don't think I can rightly name that thing." Al's drawl was more exaggerated than usual.

"Now, lemme see . . . no, I don' rightly recollect the name . . but" (brightening) . . . "if I had me an Al-ee-bammy stud horse with a blocked bladder, I'd have to guess it was a catheter for that feller!"

The young officer blushed and stalked haughtily out of the room. In a moment or two, Fireball herself came in to take over our instruction.

Fireball opened a manual and kept thumbing back and forth until she found a section on the "Wangensteen Apparatus." We had one on the ship, but I had never had any experience with it, either on the *Queen* or in any of the hospitals I had worked in. But I knew for sure who was going to get called on.

Fireball then brought out the parts of an apparatus which somewhat resembled some of the parts diagrammed in the book.

"Sergeant Copeland will now set up this device for us," Fireball decreed, "and please, no unsolicited editorial comment from any of you."

I took my time sorting out the necessary tubes, reservoirs, etc., and while I was sorting took a good, hard look at the picture in the book, and the directions. As I said, I had never used a Wangensteen before, but I did have a secret weapon of my own: I had a photographic memory when I wanted to make use of it, and boy, did I want to use it then. I took a final squint at the picture and the pieces I had sorted out, and then, as humbly as possible, announced that I always did this kind of exercise better blindfolded. Al Draper took the cue and quickly came up and wrapped a towel around my head and secured it. I sweated a little, and it took a bit of time, but my secret weapon stood me in good stead, and I put that monstrosity back together. Meeting adjourned sine die, and we went back to taking care of sick people again. Fireball took to her quarters and probably downed a double dose of Bayer, while pondering her next move.

On the last day out from New York on the return voyage an event occurred which checkmated our beleagured Fireball, and constituted what we considered a successful conclusion to the "War of the *Queen's* Medics."

A seriously ill U.S. Navy man came to the hospital. He was dehydrated, had a high fever, and bronchitis and laryngitis. His throat was swollen almost shut, he could barely breathe through his nose, and his voice had become an unintelligible gurgle. Major Freund ordered full bed rest, antibiotic injections, and round-the-clock infusion of glucose intravenously.

The case was deemed important enough for Fireball to deploy one of her coterie of nurses to administer the intravenous. I was bathing the sailor with alcohol sponges to help cool him down, but I stepped out of the way into the aisle when the nurse came in to start the intravenous. She made her set-up just fine, but with the rolling of the ship she missed the big vein. I watched, in horrified disbelief, as I saw her, in desperation, sweep the sharp end of the needle back and forth under the skin as she searched for the blood vessel. The sailor writhed in agony, as the needle cut a fresh swath each time she sought a new angle. Finally, it was more than I could take.

"My God, Lieutenant, start over again, you're killin' this guy!"

"This is where it goes," she responded.

"Pull it out! Put it in the other arm! Put it in the big vein here in his ankle," I pleaded.

She made another determined sweep in a futile effort to find the vein, which by now had disappeared from view because of all the blood pooling up under the skin. The sailor moaned and gurgled, and I moved.

I took her by the right arm, removed the needle from her hand, and told her to scram. I could only wonder momentarily if she were somehow related to my sadistic sergeant back at Brooke General, so long ago.

But that was just the thought of a moment. I found a fine big vein in the man's left ankle and started the vital intravenous flowing. Then, on the double, I got an ice bag and a roll of bandage and applied the cold pack to the hematoma she had caused, which by then had swollen to the size of a racquet ball.

I felt a tapping on my shoulder. A stern-faced Major Freund, flanked by the nurse I had forcibly ejected, was there to deal with me. The Major asked me why I had been so rude and unprofessional.

"Have a look, Major Freund," I said, as I undid the bandage holding the ice pack on the sailor's injured arm.

It was the only time I ever saw our major angry. He whirled on the lieutenant and said, "Lieutenant, you are confined to quarters except for meals for the remainder of this voyage, and you will thereafter be transferred from our ship as quickly as possible." He looked down again at the patient's arm, with an expression of horror and disbelief.

"Carry on, Copeland," was all he said.

Among the first to disembark at Pier 90 next day was Fireball Rose and her company, and those of us who watched them go were polite enough not to cheer. I often wondered, though, what they said about us in their report on our fitness to serve up healing services to the passenger troops on the *Queen*, but

Major Freund never did volunteer any information. Nor did I ever ask.

Chapter 3

THE QUEEN'S WAR

Commodore Bisset, the Old Man

This grand old man had already spent a good many years at sea before World War II, when he was assigned to the *Queen Mary.*

I never met him, but one can get a feel for a captain just by being on his ship. I used to tell soldiers who were showing signs of emotional distress, during a bad Atlantic storm, or at one of those times when we had a real U-boat scare, that they were in two sets of good hands, God's and Commodore Bisset's.[4]

Commodore Bisset enforced the rules rigidly: Air Raid Precaution (ARP) drills every day, testing the water-tight doors on D Deck daily, repeated admonitions against sneaking a cigarette on deck at night, prohibiting the hospital from using its X-ray machine because of the strong signal emitted, requiring daily lifeboat drills by key crew members and life jackets on everyone, including medics—these were some of the standard precautions he observed. And another rule rigidly adhered to was that the ship never stopped once it was underway, for any

---

4. Ed. note: The author's memory may have been faulty here. Commodore James Gordon Bisset was ship's captain for just eight of the nineteen crossings Bob made on the *Queen.* Either Bob did not realize the ship's captains changed periodically, or he mentions only Commodore Bisset in his narrative because Bisset was the subject of this anecdote.

Commodore James Gordon Bisset.

Q.M. DAILY

EDITOR: 1ST. LIEUT. RALPH BLANCHARD   OFFICE: STUDIO, PROMENADE DECK   ASST. EDITOR: PVT. JAMES C. KURZ

No. 2.   WEDNESDAY, FEBRUARY 25, 1942

"REJECT THE TURTLE POLICY"——ROOSEVELT

QUEEN MARY JIVE BAND SWINGS IT!

Calling all 'Hep Cats'! Calling all 'Jive Artists'! Calling all 'Rug Cutters'! Yes, you can swing on out to the Queen Mary Jive Band.

It all happened very casually. One evening a few of the boys were whooping it up in their cabin. Others came around with 'squeeze boxes,' saxes and clarinets and as a result we have a very sweet little music-making organization aboard.

You will hear them often during the voyage as they have played a command performance for the ship's captain at tea, played frequently in the officers' lounge and in the sergeants' room. Very soon, the band is going to play while the operators change reels at the movies.

The members of the band are Sgt. P. H. Jones, 441st Ord., guitar; Pvt. William Clark, 101st CA, Piano; Corp. S. W. Jones, 441st Ord., cornet; Pvt. John Codden, 101st CA, clarinet; Corp. Doug Avery, 101st CA, saxophone; Corp. Jolley, 101st CA, accordian; and Pvt. Ray Golden, 104th CA, clarinet and arranger.

Daily Lenten Bible Reading

*The second Commandment is:
"Thou shalt not take the name of
the Lord in vain."

The man that swearth much
shall be filled with iniquity, and a
scourge shall not depart from him."
—Eccles. 23 : 12.*

"We're going to land in England"
"We were sunk last night at three"

Are among the latest rumors That have floated out to me.

"We're headed straight for Dover"
"No, we're off for Singapore,"
"We'll wind up down in Rio"
"Or a South Sea Island Shore."

"We're going back to Brooklyn"
"To be issued quarts of grog"
"We're sailing safe as safe can be"
"In a brand new kind of fog."

From Starboard stern, to portside aft,
Rumors float on every draft.
This one from the porters' porters
That one straight from Force Headquarters.

It doesn't matter where they are,
Soldiers, Sailors or Marines.
Rumors thick and fast will fly
Where we're there are latrines.

*Harold E. McSwann.
Hq. Bty., 40th C.A. Bde Cd.at*

EXCERPTS FROM PRESIDENT'S WASHINGTON'S BIRTHDAY ADDRESS

My fellow Americans:

Washington's birthday is a most appropriate occasion for us to talk with each other about things as they are today and things as we know they shall be in the future. For each year General Washington and his Continental Army were faced continually with formidable odds and recurring defeats. Supplies and equipment were lacking. In a sense, every winter was a Valley Forge. Throughout the thirteen states there existed fifth columnists, selfish men, jealous men, who proclaimed that Washington's cause was hopeless and he could ask for a negotiated peace. The Washington conduct in those hard times has provided the model for Americans ever since; a model of moral stamina.

This war is a new kind of war. It is different from all other wars of the past, not only in its methods and weapons, but also in its geography. It is warfare in terms of every continent, every land, every sea, every air-lane in the world. The broad oceans, which have been in the past our protection from attack, have become endless battlefields on which we are constantly being challenged by our enemies. We must all understand and face the hard fact that our job now is to fight at distances which extend all the way around the globe. Until our flow of supplies gives us clear superiority we must keep on striking our enemies wherever and whenever we can meet them.

It is obvious what would happen if all great reservoirs of power were cut off from each other, either by enemy action or self imposed isolation. First, in such a case, we could no longer send aid of any kind to China for the brave people, who for nearly five years have withstood Japanese assault—have destroyed hundreds of thousands of Japanese soldiers and vast quantities of Japanese war munitions.

Secondly, if we lost communication with the southwest Pacific, all in that area, including Australia and New Zealand and Dutch Indies, would fall under Japanese domination. In such a case, could release a great number of ships and men to launch an attack on large scales against the coast of the western hemisphere, South America and Central America, including Alaska. At

the same time, she could immediately extend her conquest in the other direction — toward India, through the Indian Ocean, to Africa, to the Near East and try to join forces with Germany and Italy.

Thirdly, if we were to stop sending munitions to the British and Russians in the Mediterranean area and the Persian Gulf and Red sea, we would be helping the Nazis to overrun Turkey and Syria and Iraq and Persia, that is now called Iran, and Egypt, and the Suez Canal, the whole coast of North Africa itself and with that inevitably the whole coast of west Africa, putting Germany within easy striking distance of South America, 1500 miles away.

Fourthly, if, by such a policy, we cease to effect the North Atlantic supply line to Britain and Russia, we would help to split the counter offense by Russia against the Nazis and help to deprive Britain of essential food supplies and munitions.

Now many, fearing that we are sticking our necks out, want our National Bird to be turned into a turtle, but we prefer to remain the Eagle, as it is, flying high and striking hard. I know I speak for the mass of American people when I say we will reject the turtle policy and continue increasingly the policy of carrying the war to the enemy in distant lands and distant water, as far away as possible from our own grounds.

Some say the Japanese gains in the Philippines were made possible only by the success of their surprise attack on Pearl Harbor. I tell you this is not so. Even if the attack had not been made it would have been a hopeless operation for us to send the complete fleet to the Philippines, while all those on the island bases were under sole control of the Japanese.

Your government has unmistakable confidence that you will hear the worst without flinching or losing heart; you must, in turn, have complete confidence that the government is keeping from you only information which will help the enemy.

The United Nations constitute the association of independent people and equal dignities and equal importance. They are dedicated to the common cause. We share equally the anguish and awful sacrifices if war in a partnership of our common enterprise. We must share the shined picture which we must play our ports.

10,000-TON SHIP SET AFLAME IN BANKA STRAIT

On the western approach to the East Indies, Allied dive bombers set a 10,000 ton ship aflame in attacking a number of enemy vessels in the Banka Strait off Sumatra where many enemy reinforcements were being concentrated despite stubborn Dutch land resistance in some sectors. The enemy pincers were battered, but still jabbing steadily into the Java defense flanks, and Japanese planes ranged over the island to-day, striking primarily at air bases and the Soerabaya Naval Base in the usual pre-invasion tactics. Several enemy 'planes were destroyed.

The furious Allied air and sea assault on the Japanese fleet off Bali, which started last Thursday, bolstered the hopes of a strong stand in defense of Java. It apparently was an outstanding victory as 9 enemy vessels were sunk and 21 were damaged. Of the sunken vessels, 6 were transports, 1 battleship, 1 destroyer and 1 cruiser. The damaged vessels include 11 cruisers, 3 transports and 2 destroyers. The enemy also lost 12 bombers and 35 fighters in the way of aircraft. Dispatches made clear that it would be a mistake to regard these successes as meaning there was any change in the grav.ty to the last United Nations base in the Dutch East Indies.

NEWS IN BRIEF

BURMA.—Japanese offensive still pounding against British lines on front somewhere between the Bilil and Sittig Rivers. This front is only a matter of 13 miles from Rangoon.

PHILIPPINES.— Fighting dies down as MacArthur's forces continue stubborn resistance on Datan Peninsula.

RUSSIA.—Stalin promises that stern, hard fighting will drive the Germans from all Soviet territory.

WASHINGTON.— The first wartime 'draft lottery in 24 years will be held March 17, St. Patrick's Day. The men involved are those between the ages of 20 and 44 inclusive. The drawing will be conducted here and the historic fishbowl, which was used for draft lotteries in the first world war and the first peacetime draft, will again be brought into service.

NEW YORK.—Fred "Dixie" Walker, veteran outfielder of the Brooklyn Dodgers, ended his holdout campaign and is proceeding to the Dodgers' training camp in Havana. Pitcher Whit Wyatt is still a holdout.

An early issue of the Q.M. Daily *from Voyage #84 (the "40 days and 40 nights" voyage). You may need a magnifying glass to read it.*

reason. When one of our gunners was washed overboard during a storm it seemed unconscionable to some of the men that Commodore Bisset didn't issue orders to stop the engines and try to pluck the sailor out of the sea. But to halt the ship would have meant presenting a stationary target in mid-ocean, risking the ship and the rest of the passengers, so it was unthinkable under any circumstances. And sometimes these apparently heart-rending situations were enemy booby-traps.

Once I remember a British engineer officer came by the hospital and said we had just passed within 200 yards of a lifeboat with two very emaciated men visibly trying to get our attention. I reacted like the plowboy from Indiana that I was, stating my negative opinion of Commodore Bisset's Christian charity in the most unflattering terms. The British officer just stared down his nose at me, uncomprehending a mentality that saw only the small screen, and walked away.

But if Commodore Bisset would not risk his ship and the lives of its passengers, he was not without compassion. He kept the two men in the lifeboat in view and maneuvered the ship so that his Master-at-Arms could push off a flotation device with water and food. The sea was calm and my friend, the engineer officer, assured me that because of the "slingshot effect," whatever that is, the men in the lifeboat would be able to retrieve the flotation device, which would keep them alive until help could be sent.

The standard operating procedure after something like this occurred was to travel at least 100 miles and then radio the longitude and latitude of the lifeboat to Allied ships or planes near enough to try to effect a rescue. This precaution was necessary to prevent the enemy from zeroing in on our position. On this occasion, after we were a safe distance from the scene, this was done, and weeks later we learned that the two fellows had been rescued. How did we happen to pick up this bit of information? In one of those almost unbelievable coincidences that life sometimes presents, it turned out that one of the men in the lifeboat was the son of a *Q.M.* officer. But there was no doubt in my mind that the Old Man would have refused to stop the ship and would have traveled his hundred miles before reporting the incident if he had known that it was this officer's son out there in the lifeboat, or, in fact, if he had known it was his own son out there in mid-Atlantic in a lifeboat. One has to respect and honor such a man.

Collisions

While the *Queen* was never hit by a Nazi torpedo, she had some near misses and didn't get through the war unscathed.

In February, 1942, the big ship, crammed with U.S. troops headed for Australia, put in at Rio de Janiero for fuel and supplies. Shortly after her scheduled sailing time newscasters in Germany proudly released a statement from their Admiralty that England's pride and joy, the *Queen Mary*, had been sunk off the coast of Brazil!

But the German propaganda machine had jumped the gun.

What actually happened: a young American diplomat named John Hubner, stationed in Sao Paulo, Brazil, became suspicious when he discovered that a large radio transmitter had been imported by the German firm of Siemens and Company. He asked Brazilian police to watch the Siemens store to see who took delivery of the radio, and when a German national picked up the transmitter he was arrested. Under interrogation the prisoner disclosed the location of a Nazi radio station in the hills above Rio. The station was seized just as it was sending out a message to Nazi subs regarding the sailing time and route of the *Queen*. The Nazis sent their subs to waylay the *Queen* on her original proposed course, and were so sure of the success of their plan that they announced the "sinking" before it happened. Thanks to the alertness of Mr. Hubner, the *Queen's* course and sailing time were changed, and a terrible tragedy was avoided.[5]

---

5. Ed. note: Walter Schwider, of Naperville, Illinois, has made an intensive study of this 19,000 mile Voyage #84 from Boston to Sydney, and I am grateful to him for sending me a copy of Drew Pearson's syndicated "Washington Merry Go Round" col-

It was early in the war when the following event took place and I was not an eye-witness, but what the newsmen call "a reliable source" told me what happened, and since then it has become public knowledge.

It was general practice, always, as we approached Scotland to be met and escorted by a warship, usually a British cruiser, and the two ships would then sweep back and forth on their way into the harbor, weaving a zigzag pattern to avoid torpedo attack. In the autumn of 1942 the *Queen* and the British cruiser *Curacoa* were zigzagging, when one of the ships missed a cue and went into an irreversible collision course that ended with the *Q.M.* striking the *Curacoa* midship, breaking the smaller vessel in half. Both ends of the cruiser sank at once, drowning a reported 714 British sailors[6].

There were no casualties on the *Queen*, but her bow was badly stove in. Temporary repairs were made at the Boston Naval Shipyard, but permanent repairs had to wait until 1946 after the cessation of hostilities.

This tragedy occurred during the nadir of the Allies' fortunes, when the Nazis were pretty much in control of the air space over England; and, to prevent the damage to the public's morale that would inevitably have resulted, news of the disaster was not released until after the war.

The other time the *Queen* was involved in a collision was not so serious, and it did happen during my tour of duty. I was working in the hospital, so I didn't actually see it, but some of the soldiers who had been on deck came in afterwards to tell me about it.

Sometimes it seemed as if every time we returned to New York another maritime union had gone on strike. This time it was the tugboat operators. The *Queen Elizabeth* had arrived

umn of September 30, 1943. Mr. Schwider says that Pearson's information about Mr. Hubner and the radio transmitter was correct, but that German records obtained after the war establish that no Nazi subs were in the area when the *Queen* put into Rio, and the purpose of the Nazi propaganda was to "fish out" more intelligence on Allied troop movements.

6. Ed. note: Reports on the number of sailors who perished in this disaster vary substantially. Bob thought the 714 figure was the accurate one.

Washington Merry Go Round

By Drew Pearson

WASHINGTON. — John Hubner, young diplomat who saved the Queen Mary with around 10,000 American troops on board, has just resigned. His resignation illustrates one of the fundamental problems in keeping an alert American diplomatic service — marriage to foreign women.

Hubner is marrying the niece of the archbishop of Sao Paulo in Brazil. The state department has told him he must resign.

This means the loss of a man with many years experience, also one who proved himself especially quick-witted in a major emergency.

More than a year ago, the Nazi radio announced that the Queen Mary, crammed with U. S. troops, was sunk off Brazil. From the war department came complete silence. There was good reason for this. Here is what happened.

* * *

PLOT AGAINST QUEEN MARY - Up in Sao Paulo, central state of Brazil, Hubner had discovered that a large radio transmitter had been imported by the German firm of Siemens and Company, and was being held for delivery.

So Hubner had Brazilian police watch the Siemens store night and day to see who might take delivery. Finally, one evening a German picked up the transmitter. He was immediately arrested, subjected to stiff cross - examination, and after many hours disclosed the names of his confederates, together with the location of a Nazi radio station in the hills above Rio de Janeiro.

Hubner, working with the cooperative police, immediately rounded up the gang, and flew to Rio where the radio station was seized — just as it was sending out a message to Nazi subs regarding the sailing of the Queen Mary.

The Queen Mary had put in at Rio for fuel and supplies. She was too big to hide. Nazi agents in Rio learned her sailing time and her route and flashed this to lurking U-boats.

So sure was Berlin of this setup that it actually announced the sinking of the Queen Mary.

What the Nazis did not know was that Hubner and the Brazilian police had seized their radio station, and that the course of the Queen Mary immediately was changed.

Last month Hubner asked the state department for permission to marry a Brazilian girl. His request was refused. He resigned.

* * *

FOREIGN WIVES—Several years ago Bill Bullitt, then ambassador to Moscow, sat down to dinner in his embassy. Around the table were his staff with their wives, supposed to mingle and make friends with the Russians. They included:

(1) Counselor John C Wiley, wife is Polish and hates the Russians; (2) First Secretary Loy Henderson, whose wife is Latvian and hates the Russians; (3) Third Secretary George Kennan, whose wife is Norwegian and hates the Russians; and (4) Attache Angus Ward, whose wife is Finnish and hates the Russians.

After dinner, Bullitt got up and cabled the President that American diplomats should not be permitted to marry other than American wives. In this, he was 95 per cent right.

On the other side of the picture, however, young U. S. diplomats are not given enough time in their own country to get acquainted with American girls. They can't make love, propose, and persuade their fiances to desert their parents for an unknown foreign country, all in a three-week visit. And they don't get home more than once every four years—unless they are among the wealthy inside the state department who can afford it.

Therefore, one fundamental need in American diplomacy is to let young diplomats come home every so often for a period of a year, during which they not only can make, but also can get out in the Middle West, which really dominates the foreign policy of the United States, and see what the people are talking and thinking about.

Also the marriage ban might be relaxed somewhat, especially regarding wives from Pan American countries where the Good Neighbor policy is important.

(Copyright. 1943. King Feature Syndicate, Inc.)

Reprint of Drew Pearson's syndicated column of Thursday, September 30, 1943.

HMS CURACAO.

Queen Mary Hit, Sank Small British Cruiser

London, May 17 (U.P.).—Lifting war-long secrecy of the Royal Navy's losses in accidents and those unknown by the enemy, the Admiralty reported tonight the sinking of 163 vessels, including the 4,200-ton light cruiser Curacoa, which was rammed and sunk by the huge transport liner Queen Mary in a convoy tragedy.

The escort carrier Dasher, 10 destroyers, eight submarines and a host of smaller vessels were included in the withheld list, which brings the British Navy's war loss report up to date.

Cut Across Queen's Bow.

The Curacoa was sunk Oct. 2, 1942, when she cut across the bow of the 78,000-ton former luxury liner and was sheared in two as American troops abroad the Queen Mary looked on in horror. The small ship and its crew went to the bottom in seven minutes and only 24 of her normal crew of 400 were saved.

The tragedy occurred at 2:12 in the afternoon, 20 miles northwest of Bloody - Donegal Promontory, Donegal, North Ireland.

The Queen Mary, carrying more than 15,000 American soldiers, was

traveling at full speed toward her River Clyde dock when a lookout raised the alarm that a suspected U boat had been sighted off the port bow. The Queen Mary wheeled to starboard to take avoiding action while the Curacoa headed for the submarine, the Press Association reported.

Other ships in the delayed list comprised two armed merchant cruisers, one sloop, one frigate, three auxiliary boarding vessels, two minelayers, 13 minesweepers, 61 trawlers, 13 drifters and 29 miscellaneous craft.

The Curacoa was an anti-aircraft cruiser carrying eight 4-inch guns. The Dasher was not listed by Jane's Fighting Ships but apparently is of the 14,500-ton Archer class of escort carriers built from merchantman hulls.

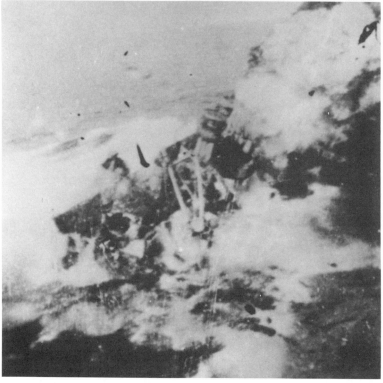

The Curacao *after being hit (top) and sinking (bottom).*

Above: the Queen at Boston shipyard after the accident showing the severe damage to her bow section.

nine days before us, carrying a full load of wounded. She was not able to get a tug within a reasonable time, and the wounded needed to be got off the ship and to hospitals, so the captain decided to dock the *Q.E.* under her own power. He was doing fine, according to my sources, but the process took so much longer than usual that the tide was beginning to ebb. To allow for this, he moved the ship sideways an extra inch or two, and in so doing managed to buckle the downstream side of Pier 90.[7] I don't suppose the Cunard people were too happy about that.

But, anyway, by the time we arrived in New York harbor, the Army had solved the problem by bringing in its own personnel to man the tugboats which were used to dock military ships. These "three-day wonders" did a fairly creditable job of keeping the traffic flowing. But sometimes their inexperience showed. On this particular day, they had obviously underestimated the heft of the *Queen Mary*—one of the tugs was using too light a cable to pull her. Suddenly the line snapped. The release of the opposing force was too much for the moving tug, which immediately upended and sank, leaving the helmsman and deckhand afloat in the icy waters of the Hudson. A small craft nearby fished them out and the 8,000 returning servicemen crowded along the fantail and port side of the *Q.M.* cheered mightily. But they cheered even louder when the waters of the Hudson suddenly exploded, and another partially clothed soldier-turned-tugboat-operator shot up from the briny depths, like a dart out of a pop gun. It must have come as a real surprise to him, finding first what a struggle it was to get the below decks restroom door open, and then traveling through water with the speed of a bullet before he had a chance to worry about pulling up his trousers.

In school he must have been one of those kids who couldn't hold it until recess.

---

7. Ed. note: Bob's account of this incident differs from that of his shipmate, Bill Roush, who says it was the *Queen Mary* which hit the pier, not the *Queen Elizabeth.*

Wolfpack

But submarines were involved in another story in which the *Queen* played a part, and this time I *was* one of the actors.

During the spring of 1945, as victory for the Allies in the European theater seemed imminent, the submarines of the Nazi navy were making desperation forays into waters close to Scotland and Ireland. Once, on a stormy night during that period the *Queen* had sailed through the submarine net, and, with her usual escort, was beginning another westbound voyage. Suddenly she did a full 360-degree turn and minutes later re-entered the harbor at Gourock.

We had almost run into the noose of a "wolfpack."

The "wolfpack" was what we called a group of four or more submarines working together in a semicircle formation. The submarines on each end of the semicircle would wait until a ship entered the target area, and then together they would close in around the ship, thus insuring a high percentage of sinkings. Fortunately, our radar had picked up four contacts in a semicircle ahead of us, and we avoided the trap.

But a British corvette was not so lucky. Immediately after we got back into the harbor, I was pulled off the *Queen* and sent with other medics on a torpedo boat to the area of the Hebrides Islands off the coast of northwest Scotland.

In due course we pulled alongside a corvette which had been torpedoed, and had been badly damaged, but had not sunk. Our job, after we boarded, was to sort through a stinking red mountain of soldiers' bodies, a conglomeration of Canadians and Americans, all armed, who had bayonnetted and knifed each other in a frenzy of fear, trying to get to the rail to jump overboard. We found a couple of men in the pile still alive, but they, too, died when we tried to move them.

That's how panic works. In the ordinary course, a few men trapped in compartments in the damaged portion of the ship would have perished, but the majority could have stayed on board and been safe, or made an orderly exodus to the lifeboats, and been rescued. Instead, the torpedo hit, the men didn't know the extent of the damage, they feared an immediate explosion, and they panicked. Some jumped into the water and were later picked up by rescue boats. But many were not so lucky. They tried to get to the rails on the area of the ship that was canted out of the water and were savagely attacked by fellow soldiers who used any available weapon to get the other man out of the way in order to save old Number One. A few lost their lives as a result of enemy action: most of them perished because of the panic of their friends.

That's why we were more concerned about the panic which would result if a torpedo hit the *Queen Mary* than we were about actual harm to the ship.

This sad tale of the corvette is another event which I never saw mentioned in the newspapers, and a special award should go to the newsmen who, if they found out about it, *didn't* report the story. In World War II there were enough horror stories of atrocities committed by the enemy to keep the public in a state of constant apprehension. To report this event at that time, demonstrating in such a graphic fashion how so-called civilized people can act, under stress, in violation of their most cherished and vaunted canons of behavior, would have done untold damage to the morale of the countries involved.

One of ours

The troops crossing on the *Queen Mary* during my time were always well-behaved, and I never had to put even a piece of adhesive tape on any soldier injured from a shipboard fight. But we never knew what might happen if we were actually attacked.

On one eastward crossing during the winter of 1945 we were about 500 miles out from the Clyde River Anchorage shortly after dawn, and "Gunsy" and his loaders were practice loading and unloading the pom-poms, sighting imaginary targets, simulating the firing process, and then repeating the exercise. Since these two gun emplacements were my first aid station during practice, I was there on duty. Suddenly I saw Gunsy hitch his harness tighter and listen intently, and then he yelled "Load!" I backed up to give those hot shell casings the right-of-way, just as one of the men inside the bridge hammered at the glass window behind my head. I looked where he pointed and saw it coming at us out of the low fog bank near the water. It looked to me to be about two miles away and BIG. The bull horn screamed:

PROBABLE ENEMY ATTACK 12 O'CLOCK, LOW TO WATER. READY ALL FORWARD GUNS. STAND BY 5-INCHER. STEADY ... STEADY."

Suddenly, veering off to our right, we saw it, a huge transport plane, clearly showing the U.S. Air Force emblem. Holy mackerel, we had almost shot at one of our own planes.

Okay, Paul Harvey, here's the rest of the story.

Aboard that transport were forty combat pilots who had finished fifty or more missions over such places as Ploesti, Omaha, Schweinfurt and Berlin, and were now en route home for well-earned R & R. They had been flying high and fast and were beginning to feel relaxed as they got beyond the range of the Luftwaffe. So when some of the passenger pilots saw and identified the *Queen Mary*, they asked the plane commander to drop down and circle us so they could get a real good look at the Queen of the Seas. That good look nearly cost them dearly—they forgot we were armed and always on the alert. It was one of the mistakes that *wasn't* made during World War II, but I heard that tempers flared between Whitehall and Washington over this episode nevertheless.

Silver balls with horns

After V-E Day we wondered when we would change from the Clyde River anchorage to the Southampton Docks as our eastern terminus. Southampton was the *Queen's* home port,

"Battle Stations!"

The Queen *at Southhampton.*

but our crew said it would take time to dredge out the channel to allow for the *Q.M.'s* 47-foot underwater draw.

The channel around the Isle of Wight had been well sown with mines by the English to minimize any attempt by the enemy to penetrate the Southampton Harbor defenses. The Solent River Channel, on the other hand, had been left free of mine fields, because it was felt no enemy subs could possibly penetrate the harbor defenses and get that far inland.

It was not until July or August of 1945 that the *Queen* was told the channel had been dredged and she could return to her home port. I remember how, as the *Q.M.* made her way slowly upstream, she scraped bottom for a brief instant. We all held our breaths, wondering whether the helmsman had got slightly offside or the dredgers had missed a stretch of silt. But then she shuddered and went on, unscathed.

It was a pleasant day, bright and cloudless. The public address system had warned everyone to dispose of their garbage before going further inland. My friend, John Bobb, and I were carrying the last GI can of disposable hospital waste to dump off the fantail of the ship. Suddenly we were thrown violently sideways and hit the bulkhead, knocking the lid off the can and dumping some of the contents onto the deck. We picked up our spilled bandages and other trash and, leaving the heavy can behind, hurried to the fantail to find out what had happened to cause the sudden pitching of the ship. A group of excited crewmen was there, hanging over the rail. One of them, seeing us, pointed down into the white water of our wake.

We saw it then, a round silver ball rolling over and over in the turbulent waters of the Solent River Channel. The thing had steel spikes called "horns" sticking out at regular intervals from its surface. It was one of the mines protecting the harbor which had somehow got loose from its moorings, probably during a storm, and evaded the safety nets. An alert lookout had given the warning, and an alert helmsman had heeded the warning instantly. Seconds lost by either could have meant disaster. Any crushing of one of the "horns" on the mine would have detonated it, and one of those mines was capable of sinking an ordinary size vessel. My friend, Harry, the Chief Master-at-Arms, told me he had seen the mine rolling in the outer edge of the six foot swath of white water along the port side of the ship as the helmsman put the *Queen* hard to starboard. A close call indeed!

When we were half a mile farther upriver we watched as a Spitfire pilot made a first high-speed pass at the floating mine to make visual contact with his target. Then he made another pass, at full throttle, and when he was about 200 feet from the mine he let go with all eight machine guns. The mine went up in a geyser of water and mist which the pilot just narrowly evaded by banking the plane. And seconds later we heard the thundering crescendo of the underwater explosion.

Further upriver the loudspeaker called attention to a peculiar looking contraption anchored in the shoreward waters off the starboard side. It was *Dumbo*, a gigantic seagoing hose-reel that had joined the invasion fleet off Normandy, and unreeled miles of huge hose that transferred fuel from tankers to the invasion beaches. *Dumbo* was a major factor in the success of the invasion, and its inventors should be acclaimed by history for their important contribution to the outcome of the war.

Another one of ours

A little personal recollection. Just after we passed *Dumbo* we suddenly saw two Spitfires coming up astern and to starboard, only about 100 feet above the water. We were carrying 10,000 replacement troops to England to relieve some of the men who were being sent home, and it seemed as if the *Queen* canted to the right as the men rushed to the starboard side of the Sun Deck, the Promenade Deck and the Main Deck to get their first look at Spitfires. The Spitfires dropped below Sun Deck level as they buzzed past, and then peeled away from each other and returned downriver again.

Many years later, when I was safety director for Indiana Refrigerator Lines, I happened to be swapping stories with some of my drivers at the Jersey Truck Center and, for some reason, related this incident. One of the men, Avery McAdams, of Modoc, Indiana, kept nodding his head and trying to interrupt me.

"Do you have any idea who those pilots were?" he asked.

"No idea at all," I said. "They buzzed us, and then they buzzed off."

Avery pulled out his wallet and showed me an old, well-worn ID card, with a picture on it. It was a much younger Avery in an RAF uniform.

"I couldn't wait," he said. "I went up to Canada and flew with the Royal Canadian Air Force until we were absorbed into the Royal Air Force after Dunkirk."

I thought, then, what a small world that war had made of our planet. Avery and I spent the rest of the evening together in the Arena Diner over coffee, re-living the European phase of World War II. Avery said he and his friend had "buzzed" the *Queen,* as fellow Americans, to salute the American troops.

But it cost him dearly: he got busted in rank for that bit of patriotic fervor.

The sappers

We had another scare on an eastbound trip in October, 1945. Around 11:00 p.m. on our first night out of New York our First Sergeant, Bill Roush, quietly but urgently awakened all of us in Cabin A143.

"Get dressed as quick as you can. Find your life jackets and report to your duty stations and begin a search for an incendiary bomb. If you see or hear anything ticking or otherwise suspicious, call the bridge immediately. We have a team of British sappers aboard, fortunately."

"Christamighty, the war's over. What's going on?" somebody protested.

Bill Roush had rarely ever given a terse order, but this time he didn't mince words.

"Get with it—NOW!"

I ran to the hospital and began my search in the operating room. Then I proceeded to the office, the broom closet and finally the wards. I went through drawers and cabinets, and felt under pillows and around and under mattresses. Only the spare ward was left. The PA system, almost in a whisper, gave the order: "All personnel, stand by!"

It was five minutes until the witching hour of midnight, when the bomb was supposed to detonate. I stood by, like a good soldier, between the operating room and the spare ward, and was wondering whether I dared go to the bathroom to relieve myself, when I heard a rhythmic clicking above my head . . . "click, click," . . . "click, click."

I dived for the phone, rang up the bridge to tell them what I had heard, and then went out on the deck, my heart in my shoes, and looked up to where I supposed the clicking sound had come from. There I saw the ship's clock, "click-clicking" away. It was setting itself forward automatically one hour for the new time zone we were entering, and after 60 "click clicks" my little bomb scare was over. But just then in rushed the squad of British sappers. They saw a Yank with a bright crimson complexion who pointed shamefacedly up at the clock. The sappers looked disgusted, shrugged . . . and slowly left.

The loudspeaker ordered the search to be continued so I went into the spare ward. Each bed had a mattress rolled up with a pillow in the center. When I unrolled the tenth mattress there was a thunderous crash on the steel deck, and I did a quick run back to the phone. I had seen what fell. It was a regular GI water canteen, but the sound it made when it crashed took it out of the "regular" category.

A rather skeptical voice on the bridge calmly assured me the sapper team would return. But he kept talking beside the open phone circuit and I could hear what he said.

"Okay, chaps . . . it's 'im again, the one who 'eard the clock ticking. Now it's a bloody canteen filled with something. Go 'ave a look."

This time the sappers trotted in through the swinging doors at a more leisurely pace. I described the terribly loud clang the canteen made as it hit the deck, and mentally cringed at the glances they exchanged with each other.

The leader knelt down by the canteen and listened intently. Apparently satisfied, and with an exaggerated wink at his comrades, he started to pick it up. It was so heavy it slipped out of his fingers, and he just managed to cushion the fall back against the deck with the palm of his hand. I saw six sappers jump in unison with me, but their reactions were as quick as their surprise. They now treated the canteen with respect, held it carefully and very gently deposited it in a pail of water.

I said we ought to just open the hatch to the boat deck and send it down to Davy Jones.

"Then we'd never know if it's real or not" the team leader said.

Then I watched while some very gutsy men played roulette with their lives as they slowly twisted off the lid of the canteen and poured out dozens of rounds of 9MM Luger ammunition. I had found a war souvenir which one of our patients had inadvertently left behind.

By way of postscript. The bomb was not on the *Queen Mary*. It was on a tanker 100 miles behind us, loaded with aviation gas destined for Europe. While we had been opening the canteen we hadn't heard the announcement over the PA calling off the search. We learned subsequently that the FBI had apprehended a suspected saboteur.

Bob Hope performing on the Queen, *probably before the war.*

Chapter 4

PASSENGERS

Bing Crosby

Often our passengers included the entertainers Uncle Sam sent over to perform for the combat troops.

I remember especially when Bing Crosby and his group traveled with us. During the trip Bing's troupe entertained the soldiers on board, but the Old Groaner was never up in front of an audience on that particular voyage, and I don't know how his manager explained his failure to appear, but the truth of the matter was that Der Bingle had a terrible case of *mal de mer*.

His ordeal began at Pier 90 when the *Queen's* 160,000 h.p. turbines started slowly edging the ship out into the middle of the Hudson River, and ended when forward motion ceased five days later in the Clyde River Anchorage in Scotland.

Of all the American entertainers who sailed with us on the *Queen Mary* Bing Crosby was probably the most beloved by the British crewmen. About halfway across the Atlantic a two-man delegation, consisting of the ship's butcher and one of the chefs, sought me out to ask if I could come down and " 'ave a look" at their hero. I asked if he was ill, and they nodded in unison.

" 'E's afraid they'll put him in the blinkin' 'ospital if he turns 'imself in, y'know," the chef said.

"Well, if 'e's sick, the blinkin' 'ospital is the plyce for 'im," I replied.

Nevertheless, as soon as I was able to get away from the ward I went to see what I could do for Mr.Crosby. I didn't find him in a VIP stateroom on Main Deck. I found him perched on the top of a mountain of 100-pound bags of potatoes in the D-Deck working alleyway which was next to the galley. This is where he had been since we left New York, and this is where he stayed for the entire voyage, except for infrequent visits to the latrine.

I hoisted my 240 pounds up to the top of his potato mountain, mashing a few spuds along the way, and introduced myself. It was obvious why the ship's crew had become so concerned. His skin color was a ghastly green and he looked severely dehydrated. I had a little trouble with the stethoscope, sorting out his chest sounds from the persistent thrum of the giant steam turbine 40 feet below, but I didn't detect anything unusual there. I had seen and smelled enough cases of seasickness to know that his acute case was complicated by another factor, but I hesitated to ask him about it, and he didn't volunteer anything when I asked about specific symptoms. But I was pretty sure my diagnosis was correct, and it was verified when I glimpsed the neck of a bottle of Seagram's poking up between potato bags.

I explained to Mr. Crosby I was only an enlisted man trained as a medic, not a doctor, and that it might be best to carry him to the hospital and let the transport surgeon look at him, but he said, "My boy, these good people give you high marks, and I don't have any notion of leaving my comfort station."

I made my way down the mountain, wondering how a man in his condition could negotiate a trip down the bags, as he apparently had, and announced to the anxious Crosby fans below that he was going to be OK. One of the crewmen went back to the hospital with me and and I gave him a few APC tablets, a giant can of pineapple juice, and an M-1 Army issue urinal duct.

"See that he gets a couple of these tablets every four or five hours, and that he drinks all the pineapple juice in the next twenty-four hours. This device" (handing him the urinal) "is for Mr. Crosby to use so he won't have to exert himself getting up and down off those potatoes. One of you guys will have to empty this . . . but not a drop is to go on the spuds, you understand?"

As soon as I could find Colonel Cohn I explained what had happened, and asked if he wanted one of the doctors to take over.

"Any chest rales?" he asked.

"None that I could hear, sir . . . but the turbines didn't have the courtesy to shut off while I listened."

"OK, check up on him later if you find time . . . Copeland, you'll find out someday, if you ever become a doctor, that one of the biggest factors contributing to the success of a patient's treatment is his faith in the person treating him . . . so I expect you're the best doctor for Mr. Crosby."

So saying Dr. Cohn went about his business.

Late that evening as I was about to turn in I remembered my famous patient, and thought I'd better check on him before bedding down for the night. I found him sleeping peacefully on top of the potatoes with two sentinels on duty at the foot of the mountain. His color and overall appearance were much improved, but the can of pineapple juice was still too full for my liking, because dehydration is what we worry about most with seasickness.

"Won't he drink this juice?" I asked one of the men.

"Oh, blimey, yes. Matter a fact 'e's been pullin' at it quite often . . . one of our blokes said 'e keeps fillin' it up with 'is other medikyshon . . . the one 'e keeps up there between the potato bags."

"Has he used the urinal?" I inquired.

"Oh, my, yes, loike you advised we've been keepin' tracks on that. See the chalky marks on the bulkhead?"

I looked at the bulkhead, and the record seemed entirely satisfactory. So I went back to my rack and slept the sleep of the contented man who knows his job well done. Peaceful and contented, except for a short dream about a bald-headed frog asleep on a mountain of empty brown bottles with a lot of green snakes crawling all over him.

The Bob Hope Show

The Bob Hope Show traveled to England twice aboard the *Queen Mary* while I was doing my tour of duty. As usual, I was too busy in the hospital and missed all the shows. But I did meet both Jerry Colonna and Bob Hope personally, and while the incidents don't prove much of anything, they are occasions I remember vividly because of the famous personalities involved.

Jerry Colonna I really met head-to-head rather than face-to-face, as he and I both tried to use the swinging louvered door on the Main Pharmacy simultaneously, but from opposite sides. We were both startled, but I was carrying an armload of empty medicine containers, and Mr.Colonna was empty-handed. My medicine containers hit the deck. Mr. Colonna apologized, which was certainly not necessary under the circumstances, and helped me pick them up. And that was all there was to that.

My encounter with Bob Hope was equally unmemorable to anyone but myself. We were mid-ocean heading east and had so few patients that trip we closed the ward just off the lab. I was therefore very much surprised one evening when I went into the lab to get a report and heard some unusual noises in the vacant ward. I opened the door and switched on the lights, and there in the center of the room stood Bob Hope!

"How in the hell do I get out of this place?" he demanded.

I said, "No problem, Mr.Hope, I was just wondering how in the hell you got in . . . you must have come through the wall."

"No, I didn't. I was outside and saw that door there and just walked in quick-like to get out of the wind and rain . . . and it closed on me . . . and there's no knob to re-open it," he explained.

And it was true. There had been a cabinet in front of that door, so there was no knob on it. We never used it as a door, and I had forgotten it was there. I escorted Mr. Hope out through the lab, and in an effort to be friendly, and perhaps also to have something to tell my grandchildren offered him a tour of our hospital.

"No thanks . . . hospitals give me the creeps!" he said, and with that, Mr.Bob Hope left my life forever.

Not so averse to what the hospital wing had to offer was the distaff contingent from the Hope show. The medics had just been assigned what we all considered rather elegant quarters in A-141 and A143. There were five of us in each room, but John Bobb and Bill Roush and I were married men, so we were not in line for the kind of fun the others were looking forward to. Our bachelor friends asked us to vacate A143 for the occasion of a party with the girls from the Hope show which Hermie from the Special Services staff was organizing. Rather grudgingly we consented, and even more grudgingly did we give permission to make trips to my "well," the 5-gallon tin of grain alcohol that had been liberated from a captured Nazi hospital and given to me.

The next morning eight rather crestfallen young men appeared at the hospital to relate their sad tale. The girls had come . . . but so had the chaperone.

Let it never be said that resourceful medics make the same mistake twice, however. Things were different on our subsequent return trip when the Bob Hope entourage headed for home. The chaperone problem was handled rather neatly. A personable young British sailor was hired to appear at the chaperone's quarters and present himself as her personal escort to the party. What he didn't know was that the location of the party on the map he was using was entirely fictitious and nowhere near the Main Pharmacy where the action was to take place. And it's easy to get lost on the *Queen*. So while the British sailor guided the infuriated chaperone from one end of the ship to the other, up and down, fore and aft, the party was in full swing behind the closed doors of the Main Pharmacy.

But again, the best laid schemes "aft gang a-gley." The medics had chosen the Main Pharmacy for the site of their party without the knowledge or approval of our Chief Pharmacist, Louis T. Macaronas. When Macaronas heard about the affair from some dirty sneak he panicked, fearing damage to his bailiwick for which he would be held responsible, so he headed posthaste for the Pharmacy to put a stop to the revelry. But the dirty sneak, ascertaining his purpose, and with a twisted sense of humor, at least so far as his fellow medics were concerned, followed Mac at a distance, telling all the homeward-bound GIs he met along the way that they were invited to a free party—girls, booze, music—all on the house. So when Mac, in high dudgeon, unlocked the door to the Pharmacy, at least fifty gate-crashing GIs followed him right into the thick of things. And the party was definitely over.

The whole affair caused lots of hard feelings among the personnel of the *Queen's* medical unit, and we never had quite the same *esprit de corps* afterwards that we had before.

But, just for the record, I was *not* the dirty sneak.

A miscellany

Mickey Rooney made the trip to England on the *Queen* in October, 1944. He particularly endeared himself to my friend, Don Trump, of Coatesville, Indiana because, always after his performances, he mingled with the troops and, always, he hit their crap games. Don said the men loved to watch Mickey's facial contortions as he rolled the dice . . . and they loved it even more because he almost always lost.

King Ibn Saud, Prince Feisal and Ali Mohammed traveled with us on their way to Washington, and they were routinely considerate about posing for my friends who had cameras.

Katherine Cornell and Sir Thomas Beecham were with us on a westward crossing in early February, 1945, but they didn't get sick so I wasn't lucky enough to meet them.

The Sikhs—we had a small group of these tall, silent, bearded men from northern India on one westbound voyage in February, 1945. A grizzled British infantry officer was in charge of them, and he walked into the hospital one night to ask if I could give him something for a couple of his men who had sore throats.

I had seen them walking the deck in their turbans and cloaks, with the British uniform underneath and a tell-tale bulge where a long curved knife hung in its scabbard. I asked about the knife.

"That knife is about all they need," the officer explained. "Oh, we give 'em grenades and machine guns and the like, but they are at their best after dark with the knives. They seem to have tremendous night vision. In the black of evening, on patrol they go like ghosts and find enemy outposts with one man awake on guard duty.

"They drop in silently," he continued, "and kill the guard. Then they bind and gag one man, and make him watch as, one by one, they brutally kill all the rest, until only that one man is left alive . . . alive, but gagged and bound so he will live to scream out the horror of it all to those who come to release him. Believe me, Rommel's Afrika Korps slept fitfully for fear my lads might come a-calling in the dead of night."

This officer and his Sikhs were bound for the Pacific Theater. I said a little prayer of thanks that the Sikhs were afraid to come to the hospital; and I think I slept a little better myself when they disembarked in New York.

The Nisei—we carried 900 of these Japanese-Americans from Pier 90 to Southampton in September of 1945. They were bound for Italy to relieve homecoming members of the 442nd, a regiment of Japanese-Americans which had set a record for being the most decorated regiment in our Army.

I was assigned the job of giving these men their yellow fever shots, and I figured for 900 it would take about five hours, since I had four men loading syringes and 100 needles with two men sterilizing them after each use.

Instead, it took all day, and even then I think some of the soldiers got away from us. Time and again I'd be down to one helper while all the others were out chasing the victims, some of them with the needles still in their arms. Japanese may be stoics using a sword to commit hari kari—I will never be able to prove otherwise—but let one of them take a good look at a hypodermic syringe and it's all over. Maybe we should have sent all our soldiers into battle against the Japanese armed with long needles.

Anyway, we must have got the majority of them inoculated, because I never heard of any epidemics. I had visions at the time of coming into port on our next trip east and seeing a huge yellow fever cloud floating over Europe. But I didn't. The most far-reaching consequence of this episode, from my standpoint, was that I had to requisition a large batch of new needles to replace the ones that had left the hospital on the arms of my Nisei patients.

The prime minister

Everyone has his Churchill stories, and I did admire the man, but frankly, I didn't much *like* him. I have to admit, however, that I never met the prime minister personally, and my dislike for him was totally irrational.

We had been told the *Queen* was Churchill's favorite ship, and, in fact, the only one he would use for trans-Atlantic crossings. Then one day we were advised that the prime minister would be among our passengers on our return trip to America which was scheduled to leave the following day. Most of our returning troops were terribly excited about the prospect of catching a glimpse of the world's most famous statesman.

The next day came and went, with no Mr. Churchill, and the following day, and the day following that. Finally, after we had sat in the Clyde River anchorage, fully loaded, for eight long days Mr. Churchill showed up. It is obviously unfair of me to judge the man's tardiness, because the scope of his obligations was so far beyond my youthful comprehension. But I wasn't thinking of his obligations or my inconvenience. I was only thinking of the 2,500 wounded and 10,000 rotation troops all loaded and waiting eight days before the voyage for home got underway. I thought for Mr. Churchill to keep these men waiting for that length of time was real crust, and I resented it on their behalf.[8]

We ran so low on hospital supplies because of that enforced layover that Sergeant Shriner had to go ashore and get two Army trucks and travel to one of our general hospitals in northern England to re-supply us.

8. Ed. note: It appears that Bob's animosity towards Mr. Churchill was un-founded. There is, in fact, no record of the prime minister traveling on the *Queen* during 1945. The delay Bob refers to may have been in early March of that year when the ship was carrying a full load of wounded and there was a lapse of nine days before turn-around on the Scottish end of the voyage. But there is no evidence Mr. Churchill was in any way responsible for that delay. Bob was still aboard the ship a year later when she left New York March 21, 1946 and Mr. Churchill, no longer prime minister, *was* a passenger. He had traveled to the United States on the *Queen Elizabeth* in January, spent some time in Florida, and given his famous "Iron Curtain" speech at West-minster College. I am indebted to Warren Hollrah, archivist at the Churchill Memo-rial, Westminster College, Fulton, Missouri, for verifying Mr. Churchill's itinerary.

Copeland, Riley and Pontzious.

Ali Mohammed of Saudi Arabia and bodyguard on their way home from San Francisco conference.

This is as close as I ever got to royalty — on the same page.

It wasn't all bedpans and bandages — we did get in a little basketball now and then. Pictured are John Bobb, the author, and Al Draper, with Al Fortmuller seated in front.

Some of the gang ready for leave. I apologize for the quality of the snapshots, but most of us weren't skilled photographers in those days and our Brownies weren't all that sophisticated, either.

Chapter 5

FRIENDS

John Bobb

John Bobb was a medic's medic. In his mid-30s when I first met him, John hailed from Ohio, and had been a funeral director before the war. He had, like me, taken his basic at Camp Barkeley, Texas and then been sent to Fitzsimmons General Hospital in Denver, Colorado for training as a medic. He was so good at what he did that the personnel officer for ship assignments at Brooklyn Army Base would often yank him off the Gray Ghost and send him on special missions. But he always returned to the *Queen*.

John, like myself, was a married man. Both of us were always trying to figure out how to get home on our three-day 500-mile passes, he to Dayton, Ohio, and I to Versailles, Indiana (100 miles more distant). Bill Roush was our sergeant, and he trusted us completely. He knew we wouldn't leave the ship until every detail was taken care of, so he always handed us our passes a day ahead of time, and as soon as we got the hospital buttoned-up, we would take off. Usually I traveled via the thumb and John took the train, but we were always looking for transportation that would give us more time at home and less on the road.

When we discovered quite by chance that we were entitled to a "Class D" priority status on military aircraft we thought we had hit pay dirt, and decided on our next three-day pass we'd make the homeward-bound trip in style.

We did. We went to Newark Airport, and signed in on the call sheet. Then we waited in the airport sitting room, patiently at first, and then with increasing anxiety, while everyone with a higher priority rating (that meant *everyone*) was called and disappeared from view through the doors to the field. We munched on candy bars and drank cold coffee that had been brewed the night before. At first we talked, and then we dozed. Finally, after we had been sitting in the airport for almost sixteen hours our names were called, and we were told we could board a plane which was sitting out on the tarmac.

The plane was a C-47 loaded with paratrooper paraphernalia. We hopped in, and it took off. Boy, it was great, definitely the way to go. And free! We were sure we'd make up the sixteen-hour delay with time to spare.

At first we did. Then we came to the Alleghenies. The plane fell a couple of hundred feet due to the action of "air pockets," or so we were told, which felt kind of like stepping off the fantail of the *Queen Mary* and landing on ice, but "not to worry," the voice from the cockpit reassured us. Then abruptly the voice from the cockpit became less reassuring.

"ATTENTION, ALL PASSENGER PERSONNEL. WE REGRET TO INFORM YOU THAT WE ARE LANDING AT OLMSTEAD AIR BASE IN MIDDLETOWN, PENNSYLVANIA WHERE YOU ARE ORDERED TO DEPLANE SO WE MAY LOAD 13,000 POUNDS OF VITAL MILITARY CARGO FOR THE WEST COAST."

So John Bobb and I were effectively deplaned, with no further hopes of getting to Dayton or Versailles, and some question about getting back to the *Queen* before she sailed. We had visions of spending the next few months in an army jail, of being busted in rank, of . . .

Well, we hung around the operations office showing our Class D priority rating to anyone who cared to look, and explaining to them the urgency of our getting back to the *Queen Mary* by sailing time. John was all for giving up on the Class D priority and giving our business to the Pennsylvania Railroad. But I was nearly broke, not an unusual state of affairs, and John couldn't handle the cost of two tickets. I suggested hitchhiking, but John said there were two things that gave him hives: egg yolks and hitchhiking.

Then our fairy godmother in the form of an operations officer told us if we could wait until six p.m. there was a U.S. Navy Transport on the ground which would be happy to fly us to Newark Airport. "Good old Navy," I thought. John and I had just enough time for a quick bite before the Navy plane was tanked up and ready to fly.

But the plane wasn't the only thing tanked up and ready to fly. The pilots had been having a jolly good time at the bar while they were waiting, judging by the fumes emitted when they boarded; and if the two of us hadn't already been strapped into our seats when the two of them hopped into the cockpit and shut the door, we probably would have opted for a charge of going A.W.O.L. rather than risking our lives with those two drunken airmen.

There may still be people around Lancaster and Palmyra who recall a dark night in 1945 when a Navy plane did all kinds of aerobatics in the wild blue yonder over eastern Pennsylvania. They may have thought, momentarily, that the enemy had invaded our skies, or our military was testing a new fighter. Actually, it was only two inebriated Navy pilots scaring the bejabbers out of a couple of midwestern farm boys, flying upside down and sideways, and maybe even backwards, I couldn't say for sure. They enjoyed themselves immensely, but I didn't, and I was wondering how many years in the brig I'd get for taking them on. I decided to wait until the good earth was underneath my feet again, though, and by that time I was really too sick to throw a punch. I did say a little prayer thanking God for getting us to Newark, and I must confess I added a request that somehow He arrange for the two of them to be shipped to Europe on the *Queen Mary*; that in due course thereafter they would both suffer emergency appendectomies; and that John Bobb and I would be assigned to assist at their operations. But some prayers go unanswered.

Side trip

Two of my classmates at Brooke General, Estil McCormick and Jeff Farley, had drawn duty at Camp Edwards in Massachusetts, and I kept getting postcards from them extolling the beauties of Cape Cod, always with an invitation to visit them.

On that particular crossing we were eight days behind on our Atlantic shuttle service because of waiting in the Clyde River Anchorage for Mr. Churchill. Even before we hit Pier 90, the staff was notified that the Gray Ghost would make a quick turnaround, and to limit passes accordingly. This meant, of course, that I wouldn't be able to go home, so I decided to take up the invitation of my friends at Camp Edwards.

I left the ship at dawn and hitchhiked from New York up to the Cape and the camp. With a little luck I found the mess hall and was able to surprise my friends by coming up behind the two of them in the chow line. Somehow their land-based chow tasted better than the stuff we had been getting on the ship; but to see my two old buddies again was the greatest. We had a lot of fun talking at breakfast, but then they had to get to work. I was going to spend the day sight-seeing, but they wanted me to go to the surgery with them instead, so we would have more time together.

Estil McCormick in civilian life was a county judge at Corsicana, Texas. Jeff Farley had been a funeral director—I don't recall exactly where he was from, somewhere in Texas—but the two of them were thirty-eight and thirty-six at the time I knew them, and the best of friends.

When we got to the hospital Mac and Jeff introduced me to some of the surgeons on the staff, explaining that I had been a classmate of theirs at Brooke General, with some added flourishes respecting my superior qualifications. One of the doctors, after shaking my hand, said, "What the hell you doin' in suntans? Go get some whites and report to #3. That way your buddies may get out of here this afternoon a few minutes early."

So I spent the whole day in surgery, and afterwards, when we were washing up, the surgeon I had been working with insisted he was going to get the CO of Camp Edwards to request my transfer to his staff. It was flattering, but I thanked him and declined as gracefully as possible. I loved the sea, and loved her chiefest *Queen* even more. I didn't think land duty could ever be as continually exciting.

Well, when we finally finished our stint in surgery my two doughty Texas friends wanted to do the town, so we set off for the bright lights of Buzzards Bay. A pooling of financial resources provided a fifth of Southern Comfort, which we took down to a pretty little park on the bay, and a few nips of the booze loosened our throats. We developed some pretty good harmony, and soon had a sizeable audience listening to three slightly-sauced soldiers doing barbershop. But then along came authority in the form of a policeman moseying our way, trying to look casual, but measuring his night stick in his hand as he approached us.

I told my Texas buddies that since I had only had a little bitty nip of the Comfort I should be our contact man. So I walked up to one of Cape Cod's finest and extended the right hand of good fellowship.

"You boys havin' a good time?" he asked, smiling.

"Well, officer, we were until we realized you might not approve," I said.

At that moment there was a swell of voices clamoring, "C'mon, Clancy, join up with the soldiers and make it a quartet."

Then for about half an hour we had a real songfest going, Mac, Jeff, Clancy and I. We went through all the old favorites, from "Sweet Adeline" to "Bill Bailey," and then started in on some of the current popular songs. Our audience loved it, and we didn't lose a spectator until I blew the whole deal when the bottle of Southern Comfort fell out of my coat pocket onto the concrete, and a half fifth of whiskey washed Clancy's legs and the leather puttees he was wearing. I thought for sure we were in for it then, and Clancy did look kind of sick, but all he said was, "Boys, don't make the mistake of throwin' that trash in the bay. Find yourselves a trash can. Otherwise I'd have to arrest you for littering."

And with that the four of us made our bows to the cheering spectators and retreated with dignity from the field. Clancy headed for home and a bath ("Me Sergeant would never believe how I got all these booze fumes on me") and we medics headed for the roller rink.

Things went rather badly at the rink—our ages totalled 102, and it had been a long time since any of us had tried to navigate on ball bearings, so we boarded a bus bound for Onset, Massachusetts and high adventure.

Things went even worse on the bus. All three of us had seats, but the bus was full when a pregnant lady got on. The little nip or two I'd had was hanging tenaciously on to my senses, so when I made to stand up to offer the lady my seat I did not so much rise as roll my buttocks around until they managed to get airborne, and at that precise moment I heard the unmistakable sound of a pair of trousers—my only pair—ripping. A protruding spring from the wellworn bus seat was the proximate cause.

The pregnant lady immediately perceived my predicament, and began rummaging in her purse. Voila! a card of safety pins. She held them up and motioned to me, so I sidled up alongside of her and she put enough pins in the back of my pants to prevent my arrest for indecent exposure, as my Texas buddies were quick to assure me.

At Onset a GI told us how to get to the Red Cross Canteen where there was a woman who fixed little things for military personnel in distress. Anyone who ever laid eyes on my derrière would agree that my problem was not a little one, but we found her, and fix it she did. By this time I only had ten hours before the *Queen* was due to sail. I knew I didn't have time to make any night spots, and my friends had another long day of surgery ahead of them. So we said goodby, and I hit the road.

I made Pier 90 in a flat time of seven hours, so bone weary I failed to note something was missing until I reached the point where a gangplank should have had a ship holding it in the air. The *Queen* was gone! I ran upstairs to the Pier Guard Office and yelled, "Why'd they leave me?

"Oh, jeez, Mac, I'll bet they're sorry about that,"—this from an unsympathetic corporal.

I hit the stairs going down like a runaway boxcar and saw a Cunard Line official getting into his Vauxhall. After I identified myself as Sergeant Copeland of the Troop Hospital he obligingly offered me a ride to the pilot boat which we both knew pulled away from the Battery pier about two hours after the gangplank was taken away from the departing ship. He told me the *QM* had sailed an hour before, which meant she had left four hours earlier than scheduled. My old friend, the pilot boat captain, "har-harred" me real good when I went scampering aboard his craft. "Told youse guys I'd get you out of a jam if you ever missed the gangplank, dint I?" And unjam me he did. We rendezvoused with the *Queen* off the Jersey coast, and I was hoisted aboard. The first and only time I ever missed a sailing.

Master Sergeant Fogarty

I met Master Sergeant Fogarty of the U.S. Army Motor Pool in London after V-E Day on my first trip to the south of England. I can't recall exactly where we met, but wherever it started out that day, it ended up in A143 on the *Queen* with some of us sipping the medication that Hermie Cohen of Special Services had concocted from my five-gallon tin of captured German grain alcohol sweetened with pineapple juice.

Master Sergeant Fogarty was one of the most powerful enlisted men in our military forces. He was a handsome, imposing figure whose Irish ancestry was evident in his good-humored approach to his own importance. In London the motor pool meant staff cars and jeeps. Once the war was over, thousands of officers were showing up at Master Sergeant Fogarty's door, day and night, with all sorts of "official" reasons for needing a vehicle. Most of them were fictitious; some were actually forged requisitions.

"They'll try anything," Fogarty complained, as he smacked his lips over our delicate blend. "This is the only way I get any peace at all. I just tell my people I'm going away for a breather, and for them not to put out any wheels unless the bearer has orders from Eisenhower himself, and then to be damn sure the general's signature isn't counterfeit."

So he took his breathers with us, and became fast friends with the *Queen's* depleted corps of medics.

Fogarty was in no hurry to go back to the States, as so many of us were. He had married an English girl, and by the time I met him they already had a little baby girl.

I asked him if there was anything I could bring him back from New York on our next trip, and his good, Irish face lighted up.

"Would you? What a fine thing if you could," he exclaimed. And so it was that every crossing we made after that some of us would go shopping for the baby necessities that couldn't be purchased in England even after the war was over. A typical list would look like this:

- 1 case of Wilson's canned condensed milk
- 2 undershirts (6 months)
- 1 dozen diapers
- Rubber pants, if available
- 6 nursing bottles
- 6 nipples for same
- 2 bars, gentle baby soap
- 1 bottle baby oil

Sergeant Fogarty never asked for anything for himself or his wife, but we managed to slip a few things in now and then for them, too.

Moon Mullins

I made another acquaintance before we sailed from Southampton the first time we docked there after the war. This one was a tech sergeant in charge of supplies named "Moon" Mullins, a native of Louisville, Kentucky. He came wandering into the hospital one day as we geared up for embarkation. He was part of the 14th Port Detachment (Southampton was designated 14th Port), and had been around for a long time. But he said he had never been on one of the big transport ships, and just wanted to tour the one he'd heard most about, the *Queen Mary*.

Talking to Moon was like talking to folks from Switzerland County, Indiana, and I promised him a tour of the ship the next time we hit port, since there wasn't time before we sailed that day. Moon hung around for awhile, until we started taking on wounded, and then left, saying, "Anytime you need anything, just let me know," to which I replied, "I'd settle for a good cup of coffee." (Most of us had switched to tea because we didn't like the chicory-laced coffee which was served on the *Queen Mary*.)

It was a throw-away line, and I had forgotten both Moon and our parting remarks until our next time in Southampton nineteen days later. I was walking past the bomb-pocked structures that housed the 14th Port Detachment when I heard a familiar voice yelling at me from the second floor of the building.

"Didn't you say you'd settle for a good cuppa coffee?" he asked.

"Yeah. Hi, Moon, how ya doin'?" I hollered back.

"Heads up, Cope, here it comes!" he said, and down came a whole case of Nescafé out of the second floor window. Somehow I managed to catch it before the box splattered on the pavement.

Moon grinned. After that we saw a lot of him, and he became kind of an honorary member of our QMMC (*Queen Mary* Medics Club). More about Moon later.

Nicky Brodsky

The first time John Bobb and I were in London we met Nicky Brodsky. We were sauntering in a residential section of the city and had stopped to look at a fenced-off area around a huge bomb crater which contained a live bomb that the sappers had not gotten to yet. We noticed a fellow tinkering with a tiny car parked at the curb. With the lack of formality bred by the war he came over to us and shook hands.

"Hello, my friends," he said in a deeply accented voice which I took to be East European, "I'm Nicholas Brodsky," and then after a few more minutes of conversation he said, "I live here in this building. Won't you come in?"

We were ushered into a beautifully-furnished apartment, dominated by a piano, and containing all kinds of other musical instruments. Nicky, it turned out, was a songsmith, a native of Hungary. He introduced us to another occupant of the apartment, one of his countrymen, Alex Paal, who was either a producer or director for Gaumont Pictures, a film company that made most of England's motion pictures at that time. The two Hungarian friends were total opposites in appearance and mannerisms. Alex Paal was brawny, aggressive and ebullient. He could have passed for a New York longshoreman. Nicky, on the other hand, had the delicate features, gentle ways, and preoccupied expression one might associate with a musician.

Nicky invited John Bobb and me to stay for tea, and during the course of a delightful afternoon confided that he was trying to emigrate to America. He said his lifelong ambition had been to write music for Hollywood; and then he talked of Josef Pasternak, another Hungarian, who was living in Cleveland, who had promised, through an intermediary, to help Nicky get to the States. I think he said Pasternak was directing a symphony orchestra in Cleveland at the time. I mentioned that I frequently hitchhiked across Ohio, and John Bobb told Nicky he was from western Ohio. When we finally left I was carrying an envelope containing a letter to Josef Pasternak and some documents, perhaps a birth or baptismal certificate, or whatever was used in Hungary in the early years of this century to record one's entry into the human condition. I promised to mail the envelope in Ohio if I was able to hitchhike home that trip, or if not, to mail it in New York. Actually, I did better than that. I caught a ride on the Pennsylvania Turnpike with a war plant "expediter" who was going to Cleveland. I called Mr. Pasternak, and his chauffeur met me on the outskirts of the city, and I gave the envelope to him.

A couple of trips intervened before any of us from the Gray Ghost were able to get up to London again, but when we did we were welcomed by Nicky Brodsky just as enthusiastically as before; and thereafter, whenever we were in London, Nicky's apartment became a home-away-from-home for John Bobb and Al Draper and me.

One time in particular I recall. Al Draper and I had returned to Southampton from London where we had delivered some baby supplies to Mrs. Fogarty and had stopped for a couple of hours at Nicky Brodsky's. Al suggested that Nicky put some of his music together and he would deliver it to Gilbert Miller and the French Music Publishers in New York. Nicky thought this was a good idea, so we carried a paper parcel full of music with us when we headed back for the ship.[9]

It was almost midnight when we got to Southampton and walked down High Street towards the docks and into the 14th Port Area. Suddenly from the corner of my eye I saw some-

---

9. Ed. note: Nicholas Brodsky did get to Hollywood, and as many people may remember, was a great success there. Perhaps his biggest hit was "Be My Love," sung by Mario Lanza in "The Toast of New Orleans" (1950), but he also wrote such favorites as "I'll Never Stop Loving You," "Love Me or Leave Me," and "Because You're Mine." He died in 1958.

thing hurtling towards us from a space between two old buildings—the something headed straight for Al's head. I leaped over him and deflected what turned out to be a two-by-four piece of lumber, but in so doing caused both of us to crash down on the cobblestones, scattering Nicky's music all over the street. I caught a glimpse of a figure between the two buildings fleeing in the opposite direction, but we couldn't give chase— we had to find and pick up all of the sheets of music.

Southampton in those early days after the war was not a particularly safe place. This was true of many major seaports, perhaps because deserters seemed to gravitate to the anonymity to be had where many nationalities were likely to be found. We had been gone only nineteen days on our last crossing, but sixteen murders had occurred in the general area of Southampton during our absence. We had been warned never to walk alone at night, but I thought that warning applied to everyone else, not to me.

The night before sailing I got hungry and saw no reason not to satisfy my craving at the Red Cross canteen. Servicemen didn't seem to hang around the canteen late at night anymore. This particular night there was just myself and the little old lady who ran the place. She fixed me a king-sized sandwich, which I washed down with several cups of good coffee. It was closing time after I finished, so I told Mrs. Chester "good night" and began the two-mile hike back to the *Queen*. I really needed to go to the restroom, but Mrs. Chester was tidying up the men's room, so I put it off.

I hadn't gone too far until my bladder screamed for relief, so I turned into an alleyway between some bomb-damaged buildings for privacy. Just as I was going to unzip I either sensed, or heard, a movement inside the darkness of the wrecked building behind me. As I turned around to investigate, a piece of wood ripped down across my right brow and glanced off my shoulder. Instantly I was surrounded by three British sailors who were pulling and striking and tearing at me and my clothes. It happened so fast, the whole affair was like a silent movie, no words were spoken at all. One assailant was busy tearing at my hip pocket and the others were trying to choke me with my own necktie. I kept attempting to orbit around so I could get a good whack at one of them, and finally I was successful. My fist connected with his belly, knocking him backwards and out of the action, but I hit him squarely on a big metal belt buckle and got some bleeding knuckles as a consequence. My assailants took off and were out of sight before I could get myself together enough to give chase. Needless to say, I walked the rest of the way back to the ship in the middle of the road, and the next time I had a craving for food after nightfall I settled for whatever was available on the *Queen*.

The bombardiers

In the autumn of 1945,when we were using Southampton Docks again, little boys who had access to the dock area would call up to the men on the ship and the ship's personnel would throw coins down to them on the dock apron, usually pennies. The kids would have a free-for-all, scrambling to get the coins and then wrestling with each other to keep them or take them away. It was really a game with the boys, and we all enjoyed watching them.

Then the British stevedores got into the act: they waited for the kids to retrieve the pennies, and then muscled in and took the money away from them. In A143 we were incensed. In A141 Pontzious, Red Stewart and Ed Nash were furious. Ed Nash did more than get angry: he came up with a lovely strategy, and after consulting with us in A143 Ed and Red Stewart went down to tell the kids their part in the plan.

"When you hear the whistle, give the coins to the dock hands and scram. You'll get the money later, we promise. Just beat it when you hear the whistle. But you gotta keep mum."

First Sergeant Bill Roush was at the porthole in A141 with the whistle. Al Draper was up on Boat Deck with a bag full of English pennies. John Bobb, Leonard Griffin, Pontzious, Stewart, Nash and I were in A143. We were the bombardiers.

Pontzious, Stewart, Nash and Copeland were filling the bombs. John Bobb and Leonard Griffin were standing on my bed beneath the porthole, each of them holding one end of a towel. High aloft on Boat Deck, Draper seeded the dock with a few well-aimed pennies. The kids began scrambling for them, and the stevedores immediately descended on the boys to take them away. At that precise moment Bill Roush blew the whistle and the kids ran away, leaving the dock hands fighting each other for the money which Draper was doling out sparingly, and then

BOMBS AWAY!

Our government-issue condoms were made of fine, strong rubber. They would hold about two gallons of water, making a very sizeable sphere when loaded. The towel was a tolerably efficient launching device. We were able to drop three bombs with devastating accuracy before the crowd dispersed the first time. Then the kids came back, and the routine was repeated. The stevedores couldn't figure out where the water was coming from, but finally after a few successful "bomb runs" they got smart and put out a spotter. When Leonard and John saw him pointing up to A143 and realized that our cover had been blown, they got a bit jittery and missed the porthole the next time, causing a premature explosion—on my bed.

Then the crowd below dispersed, but we had accomplished our mission, what the professionals might call "saturation bombing." You've never seen anyone wetter than those dock hands. Or madder.

But the bombardiers had to disperse then, too. The stevedores had boarded the *Queen* and were searching the ship for the bombing crew. We found sanctuary in various secluded areas, Al Shriner's supply room, the laboratory, even the broom closet.

None of us got caught, and they didn't find my water-soaked bed, but I did have to sleep in the hospital for the next three nights. It was worth it.

Bombardiers

Staff officer "Jack" Greene.

Back row: Copeland, Shriner, Wrablik, Nash, Stamberg (?). Front row:
Miller, Draper, Griffin, Stewart.

The best damn sergeant in the
U.S. Army.

Ray Neale

Ray Neale was the *Queen Mary's* steward on A Deck. He was slightly built and quietly efficient, and had a real affection for the American medics, which we reciprocated. His home in Southampton had been bombed, so his wife, Jean, and their two children lived with his parents in their old brick house which boasted only one small coal-fire grate. During the war, when we were docking in Scotland, Ray didn't get back to see his family more than once a year, but after V-E Day when the *Queen* made Southampton her home port again, we were often invited to spend an afternoon or evening in the Neale's home. So when Ray got the scuttlebutt that the *Queen* was due to be in Southampton over Christmas, 1945, he invited some of the medics who were particular friends of his to spend Christmas Day with his family.

There were five of us who were invited, Bill Roush, John Bobb, Blake Miller, Leonard Griffin and I. We all did some preparatory shopping in New York. I bought mustard, spices, canned meat, cake frosting, and a fifth of Jack Daniels, things which were non-perishable and would keep, but which were not generally available then in England.

Ordinarily there was a friendly twosome at the Customs exit who knew us and would tip their hats and wave us through. On this Christmas Day, however, there was a crew of the meanest looking British Customs fellows ever assembled. Either they were angry about having to work the holiday, or they were all fathers of British girls who had been wronged by Yankee soldiers. In any event, they were *not* friendly, and they did *not* wave us through. Instead they ordered us into the Customs shack and made us empty all our pockets and musette bags.

Blake Miller, who had an honest Pennsylvania coal-miner face, got turned loose first. He only had an undeclared box of cookies, anyway. Then they let John Bobb through with his sugar and sardines. I don't recall what Bill Roush had, but he was permitted to leave, which left only Leonard Griffin and me. I knew I was in for it with my undeclared bottle of Jack

Daniels, so as Blake and John went out of the shack I let loose with a barrage of oratory. The English were truly fair weather friends, I said, taking all our freely offered American assistance when they needed it, and then turning on us when the crisis was over. Was this why I had worked my tail to the bone taking care of their English prisoners of war returning home from Japanese prison camps, and almost been killed by one of them? Where was the comradeship of the war years? Why were we treated like criminals when we were only taking some sippin' whiskey and nylon stockings (Leonard's offering) as Christmas presents for some kind English people who had invited us into their home for the holiday? Thank God not all Englishmen were so insensitive and unappreciative as you Customs blokes, but go ahead, divide up my things among you and write my wife and tell her I'll be in Wormwood Scrubs for a few years. Obviously it's not going to bother you fellas that she'll have to go to work on her hands and knees scrubbing floors in a canning factory to support our two little boys. And so forth, and so on. I was beginning to feel the true pathos of the situation myself.

Leonard Griffin told me later the Customs guard giving him the once-over, as if talking to himself, said "Blimey, 'e and the P.M. must've 'ad the sime elly-cution teacher." Maybe it was my harangue, maybe not. Whatever, they suddenly decided to let us go and Leonard and I made tracks to catch up with our buddies.

That Christmas Day was memorable. Jean Neale had fixed a traditional dinner with roast beef, Yorkshire pudding and plum duff, among other things. And Ray Neale had some secret source for procuring wine, which he had been hoarding for the occasion. We had a choice of seven different varieties of wine or ginger beer, and we tried them all, before, during and after the meal. I had never been a drinker and didn't realize the wallop wine can pack. I remember standing outside in the afternoon holding both hands against the brick house trying to keep it braced up. Or perhaps it was the other way around. I don't really remember this, of course. I only know I kept that house from falling down because one of other fellows had a camera with him and took some incriminating photographs.

I had my first and last hangover the next day, but it was all worthwhile—the Neale's got their sippin' whiskey.

The Ray Neale Family, Christmas, 1945; 98 Bittern Road, Southampton, England.

And their Christmas dinner guests: (from left to right) Bob Copeland, Blake Miller, John Bobb, Bill Roush, Leonard Griffin (?)

John Bobb

Bob Copeland

Al Draper

Len Griffin

Our resident artist, Otto Wrablik, drew these cartoons as a Christmas gift from all of us for our sergeant, Bill Roush.

Louis Macaronas

Blake Miller

Dean Reilly

Al Shriner

Bill Stamberg

Red Stewart

Oliver Wrablik

Chapter 6

SPECIAL PEOPLE

Lt. William A. Flett

When I first went aboard the *Queen* I expected to be assigned to the operating room staff, and I really felt let down when I found I was "outranked" and was scheduled for more mundane duty.

But if I had been assigned to the surgery I probably would never have met nineteen-year-old Bill Flett on that first return voyage.

In the hospital, as we changed soiled bandages and clipped away the last vestiges of toes that had been frozen, we heard from the patients about things like "bouncing Betties," "teller mines," "potato mashers," and the terrifying "88's."

The Nazis had developed the 88-millimeter cannon to the point where it could fire at a single soldier with deadly accuracy and the spraying effect that the GIs called a "tree burst." Bill Flett had been in the front lines in France for three days when a "tree burst" came his way, and twenty-two small fragments of hot steel riddled his skull. The field hospital surgeon did what he could to remove some of the fragments, and then shipped him back to England. Instead of being sent to an English hospital his litter was taken aboard The *Romsey* on its last trip before the *Queen* was scheduled to sail at sunset for New

York. Our reconaissance planes had already left to scan the coastal area along our westbound path. Farther out in the Irish Sea a warship was circling, waiting to escort us through the danger zone. Bill was on the last stretcher to be taken aboard, and I suppose the doctors decided to send him home because they felt his case was hopeless anyway.

In those days we didn't keep much in the way of medical records, mainly because there weren't enough of us "treaters" in relation to the number of "treatees." One could only guess how long it had been since that shell had exploded in Bill's head: how long he had been on the battlefield before he had been found; how long he had been at the field hospital; how long it had taken for him to be carted out of France and across the Channel; and, finally, once in England, how long it had taken for him to be transported across the country, north and west along England's war-ravaged and bumpy roads, until he finally arrived at Gourock Docks. The stench of the blood-stained bandage wound around his head indicated it must have been a very long time indeed.

I knew, anyway, as soon as I saw him, that it had been a good many days since he had passed any urine. I could tell by his swollen bladder, which was so distended it would have been horribly painful, impossible to bear if his brain had not been so traumatized it probably wasn't responding to pain signals.

We had seventy-eight other seriously wounded patients who needed immediate attention. The only thing I had time to do for Bill Flett was to catheterize him and relieve the pressure of the backed-up urine before permanent damage was done to his organs. When I inserted the catheter, the pressure was so great that the urine gushed up to the deck head (ceiling) in Main Deck 241, and was so dark with blood that it left a permanent stain on the painted metal.

Bill's only sign of being alive was a slight movement of the eyeball. I made a silent vow to change his bandage before I quit work the next morning, but we had those seventy-eight other patients to look after, and we only had five medics on the night shift in that section of Main Deck to care for all those men:

Army Nurse Ann Shipman, Al Draper, a young man we called
"Shorty," myself, and another fellow whose name I cannot recall and will therefore refer to hereafter as the "Nameless
One." He was one of our "spoiled brats," always bemoaning the
fate that had assigned him to the medical service, and useless
except for running errands. He had been in the military police,
and I, for one, wished the MPs had hung on to him.

But Lt. Shipman and Al Draper were both competent, dedicated medics. Lt. Shipman, was a fine nurse, only weeks out of
school and proud to be in the Army Nurse Corps. What Al
Draper may have lacked in medical training he made up for
with his good humor and his ability to communicate with the
men. Al stayed with us for a few voyages, then was transferred,
and then was sent back to us again. I always felt good when Al
was on the staff.

"Shorty" had been a mail clerk at an Army Post Office. He
was a reluctant recruit, but subject to being influenced. I gave
him a little talking-to that first night out of Scotland, and
never had much trouble with him afterwards. If he hadn't been
transferred when we hit shore I probably could have made a
decent medic out of him.

It was thirteen hours and hundreds of miles later before I
got around to Bill Flett again. I took Shorty with me, and some
surgical supplies, and went to Room 241 where Bill had been
put on the top bunk in the single bed room; the wounded man
in the lower bunk was sound asleep. I went to work on the
bandage. I had to be very careful in removing the dressing not
to take away pieces of scalp and tissue with it. It took a long
time, working very painstakingly with scissors and alcohol and
cotton swabs and soap and water, to clear away the stinking
gauze, and I was pleasantly surprised that Shorty was behav-
ing so well. Finally I was able to pull some of the last gauze off
the skull itself, and to reveal part of the open wound.

Suddenly I heard an explosive gutteral sound. I looked over
at Shorty, whose eyes had become glazed. With a last, desperate effort he shoved the wash basin towards me and fainted on
to the steel deck, lacerating his own scalp in the process. Then

I had to take time out to bring Shorty back to consciousness, and wrap a tight bandage on his wound. I sent him back to Lt. Shipman for re-assignment to other duty, and asked her to send me the Nameless One on the double.

The Nameless One, to my surprise, came quickly, and before he had to look at Lt. Flett's head I tried to prepare him for his job and tell him exactly what he was required to do, which was to hold the instruments, basin and bandages and hand them to me when I needed them.

My ploy didn't work. It was a bad night off northern Ireland anyway, and the ship was rolling and pitching more than usual. As soon as Nameless One saw poor Bill's partially unwrapped head, he vomited copiously all over the patient, my arms, the other patient still sleeping peacefully below us, and the deck.

"What am I doing here?" he wailed.

"I'll tell you what you're doing here," I answered, disgusted. "You're leaving. GET OUT!"

I set to work to clean up the vomitus and replenish my supplies, and was finally able to get back to what I had begun, the job of cleaning and re-bandaging Bill's head. All the time I was working I kept trying to get some response from Bill, but there was no reaction at all. Transport Surgeon Colonel Cohn picked that particular time, when I had just finished bandaging Bill, for an inspection tour of our ward. It was now about 7:00 a.m. I had been on duty continuously since 4:00 p.m. the previous day, and was totally exhausted. In his very gentle way Colonel Cohn mentioned seeing some unemptied urinals in the corridor, but he must also have seen how worn out I was, because he just said he'd ask someone to take care of them for me. I should have explained to him why the ward was not shipshape, but by that time I was too tired to find the energy which it would have taken to furnish an explanation.

Four more nights passed before we hit New York harbor (the *Queen* always managed to arrive in the daytime hours). Each of those nights I found time to give Bill Flett a little extra attention: an arm and leg massage, an alcohol rub, a cold pack for his head. Finally, towards the end of our trip I noticed a little progress. Bill rolled his eyes, wiggled the fingers on one hand and, miracle of miracles, he even managed to speak a few monosyllables. I put on a fresh bandage for his homecoming. I never saw Lt. Flett again, but I know he lived. About five years later I received a letter from a lady who said she was Bill Flett's mother. She thanked me for what I had done for Bill, and said I was responsible for saving his life. Apparently, Bill recovered enough to work in some capacity for the Pepsi Cola Company. I don't know how she ever found me in Indianapolis, but her letter certainly gave my spirits a lift at a time when I really needed it. As for saving his life, I didn't. I am sure she knew Who did.

Herman Ephraim Cohen

I guess if there was one man I met on the *Queen* whom I genuinely disliked, it had to be Herman Ephraim Cohen (pseudonym).

This fellow did as nearly nothing as it was possible to do . . . a typical rich kid attached to the U.S. Army Special Services who had gotten himself a cushy job, traveling back and forth on the *Q.M.*, arranging entertainment for the troops while they were on board. He was a man who seemed to make an art form out of gold-bricking. Fortunately our paths didn't cross too often, but when they did I'm afraid I didn't make much effort to disguise the contempt I felt for him and his kind.

Herman was the offspring of a marriage between members of two great European banking families, both of them high on Hitler's hit list. They had left Germany in the 30's, and Hermie got his education at Christchurch, Oxford. I didn't have this information then, when I found his attitude so distasteful. I only learned it after the war when I met up with an old comrade of those years, and in the course of our reminiscing learned how completely Hermie's "spoiled-little-rich-kid" act had deceived all of us, but especially me.

The truth is that Hermie continued to work secretly all during the war training CID and OSS men to operate behind enemy lines, most of his one-on-one instruction being done, unbeknownst to any of us, of course, on these *Queen Mary* crossings.

Some of these CID and OSS men who penetrated the Nazi fortress by parachute or rubber boat or on foot got their final polish from Hermie. They went into Norway and the Netherlands and France, and even into Germany itself, to assist the underground with knowledge of things like whose aunt was married to General Von "So-and-So," and whose money was tied up in what bank; about family illnesses and food preferences and social standing and extra-marital affairs; and 1,001 other tidbits of information that could prove useful to underground agents who were gambling their lives if they guessed wrong about someone.

This helped to explain, after all those years, an incident during my *Queen Mary* days that had always remained a mystery.

We were anchored in the Clyde River beginning to load wounded. I had been up most of the night bringing those heavy mattresses up from the hold, but knocked off work around 3:00 a.m., totally exhausted, and fell into my canvas rack fully clothed except for my shoes. It seemed I had only just fallen asleep when a strong hand was shaking me, and through the fog of sleep I kept hearing a voice repeating my name over and over.

"Copeland! Copeland!"

There was an imperative that finally penetrated my slumbering psyche.

"Yes, sir," I mumbled groggily.

"Barrington here, Copeland, of the ship staff, and directing this 'ere officer to you."

Seeing a full "bird colonel" with a .45 strapped on him, I jumped out of the canvas with alacrity. It was shortly after I had been cleared of the charge of "giving aid and comfort to the enemy," and I was sure I was under arrest again. The colonel assured me I was not, and told me to put on my shoes and something warm, and to come with him. He said my superiors had already been notified.

Still half asleep I fell in beside him as we went over to the shell door and out on board a launch. Someone ran up and threw a heavy medical kit out to me, and we sped off in the gray dawn, headed towards shore.

The colonel was not unfriendly, but neither was he communicative. We left the launch at Gourock dockside and stepped into a waiting army sedan with motorcycle escort. Minutes later we came to an airstrip where a sleek-looking aircraft was waiting with engines idling.

As the driver of the sedan hurled my kit and a Stokes litter through the bomb bay of the aircraft, the colonel said quietly, "You are making an important trip. Do the best you can to accomplish your part of the mission. I'm going to ask you now to raise your hand." And I was then sworn to secrecy concerning any conclusions I might draw as to the purpose of the mission. He wished me "Godspeed," and pushed me towards the door of the plane. The last words I heard, as the plane engines revved up were hardly reassuring: "You better deliver! I picked you myself!"

I found myself inside a strange plane partly made of laminated wood, especially the fuselage. Strange suspension devices, and what appeared to be bomb release doors, were in my way as I tried to get up front to greet the other two occupants, who were obviously co-pilots. One of them yelled, "Hang on, matey, no place to buckle you up!"

We were airborne almost immediately. I finally made my way forward, and began asking questions, trying to find out what the deal was. They were both Canadians, first RCAF and now RAF, and both had the same first name, "Eric." They didn't seem to know much more than I did about our mission, except that they also had been roused before dawn, and had been given brief starting instructions together with a sealed envelope which was to be opened as soon as we cleared the east coast of Scotland. They told me that I was riding in a "Mosquito," which according to the two Erics was the fastest plane on earth, capable, they said, of traveling better than 500 mph.

It seemed only about five minutes before we shot out over open ocean, and at this point they quit talking and dropped down to just feet above the water, and that's the way we traveled until landfall.

Meantime, one of the pilots had opened the envelope and, motioning me to huddle with them, he read that we were to proceed on a described course to what he called a "coordinate," to land at an airfield so many kilometers beyond the Rhine, to refuel, to board a badly wounded man, and to return as speedily as possible. We were to take any evasive action deemed necessary to bring the operation to a successful completion.

I asked Eric One what country we were flying over, scaring the cows and an occasional farmer.

"Holland," he replied.

"Where's Belgium?" I asked. He pointed south, and then it dawned on me that we were headed southeast into Hitler's own ballpark. I asked what kind of armament we carried, and Eric 2 squirmed around in his seat and pulled a little pistol holster out of his pocket.

"38-caliber," he grinned. "We have a couple of things on the plane we should shoot up if we crash, you know, so the enemy won't find out what makes the Mosquito sting."

The next few minutes I heard the Erics talking about landmarks they remembered, and I realized they had been in on the destruction of some hydroelectric dams in Germany that devastated Germany's war production, and that this Mosquito was the plane which delivered the land mines which did the job. The blinding speed of this plane had allowed "skip bombing" at low altitudes and rendered enemy flak towers virtually harmless.

They were able to pinpoint the airfield we were looking for shortly after we passed over the Rhine, but a spurt of black smoke in the sky just ahead of the cockpit showed that not everything was "all tidied up and tickety-boo" as General Montgomery once said.

We had overshot our landing spot, and in circling, went right over a Nazi anti-aircraft position which had not yet surrendered. But the Mosquito was too fast, they couldn't get a fix on us. Down below on the airfield where we were supposed to land an armored bulldozer had not yet finished levelling out the bomb holes in the runway, so we circled wide on the first overrun to give the dozer crew more time. There was a battery of big guns down below us, which the Erics identified as our own 155's, placed snugly in a drainage ditch, and the runway where we were to land was smack-dab between those 155's and the German Army which was east about four or five miles.

We kept circling low and as far west as feasible until a gunnery officer stopped the gunfire, ran out on the runway and waved up at us, indicating their readiness for us to land. It is a tribute to the skill of the two Erics that the Mosquito held together when they put her down. The runway was soft from the bulldozing, and dirt and rocks clattered up against the plywood belly of the plane with tremendous force. But she did not seem to be damaged.

As quickly as we could, we piled out. I saw the gunnery officer talking excitedly to the two Erics, pointing to the muzzles of the 155's. Eric One came running up to me and shouted, "They've got orders to keep shooting. Can you load your man under those conditions?" I told him I would do my utmost, and hoped the patient could stand the stress.

Within minutes an Army truck full of GI gas cans stopped at the nose of the plane, and three soldiers and one of the Erics began fueling the Mosquito out of the cans. A Jeep with a platform for carrying wounded rolled up to the door of the plane where I was standing, and a captain with a stethoscope began loosening the straps on the litter carrying the wounded man. Together, and as gently as possible, we transferred the wounded man to the Stokes litter and put him in the plane. Meanwhile, about 300 feet in back of us, the 155's began blasting away, and dirt and rocks were flying all around us, a storm of debris from the air currents created by the firing of the guns.

"Those damn guns are making such a racket, I can't tell whether he's still alive or not," the captain shouted over the din." Here, you see if you can find a heartbeat."

I couldn't find a heartbeat either, but I felt his pulse, and it was altogether satisfactory, I thought, for a man who was so swathed around the mid-section with heavy blood-stained bandages. About then I noticed blood on the stethoscope's ear pieces as I handed it back to the captain. I ran a finger into my right ear, and it came out bloody. Then my nose started bleeding, and we hurried a little faster. The concussion from the 155's was getting to my tender parts. I wondered momentarily about where else I might be bleeding; but I was most concerned about what damage it would do to my patient.

The captain told me his unit had seen this man being gunned down by Nazis as he tried to break past their lines to get over to our side. It had happened the preceding evening, but it was about midnight before the medics could get to him. Meantime, various front line units had been getting inquiries from High Up asking about a man getting through from the other side. And finally, putting two and two together, they decided this badly-wounded man was the one the brass were so concerned about.

The patient looked to me like anyone else who is about to meet his Maker, and I would have thought this whole dangerous evacuation effort was an exercise in futility except for that strong pulse I had detected.

The captain admonished me to avoid disturbing the patient's bandages under any circumstances. The only medication, he said, had been a couple of Syrettes of morphine and continuing infusions of plasma.

"Try to avoid hemorrhaging, if at all possible, and if he regains consciousness, he'll probably need more morphine." I saw him eyeing my well-stocked medical kit.

"See anything you want to liberate?" I asked.

He snatched about 50 Syrettes of morphine, leaving me two, and hopped in his Jeep.

"I wish to hell we were through here, and I could go back with you," he yelled as he waved goodbye.

I had my patient secured, so I jumped out to see how much longer the re-fueling would take. I saw the men on the fuel truck stowing away the empty cans, and Eric 2 said as soon as we could get the 155's to stop firing we'd take off. He ran out to get the gunnery officer's attention, and I asked the Jeep driver if the medical officer was with his outfit.

"Say, Mac, you just rubbed elbows with the goddamnesdest bravest doctor in this war. He ain't scared of nuthin'."[10]

As soon as the guns stopped, we took off. Again, there was that horrible noise under the Mosquito's belly, from flying rocks and dirt. This time we didn't cross over any enemy ack-ack, and almost before I realized it we had cleared the coast of Holland, and were flying out over the North Sea.

When I looked at my watch it was only 10:15 a.m.!

I was busy with my patient during the homeward trip, and didn't have time to chat with the pilots. But just before we roared in over the Scottish coast I thought I heard the Erics talking about the landing gear.

I yelled up at them, "What happened, did we tear it off back there?"

Eric One turned around in his seat.

"Listen," he said, "we're in the dark about that. We can't tell. There's a chance it's damaged and might collapse. We'll go in as gentle as we can, but we have to land at about 150 mph."

Ten minute later we were on the soil of Scotland. The landing gear held up.

There was quite a gathering outside the plane door. All I had to do was stand back out of the way. Someone else did the lifting for a change. In seconds, my wounded man was on the ground being attended to, listened to, and then carefully trans-

---

10. I am sure this was Captain Pete Suer whose death is chronicled in the *Saga of the All-American (History of Airborne Soldiery)* (privately published), as having taken place that winter while he rode the front bumper of a Jeep looking for a wounded man. Caught in the middle of the lines, with both legs shot off, lying out for several hours in severe cold, he died before rescuers could get to him. I wish, too, that he could have gone back with me that morning.

ferred into a regular Army ambulance and driven away. There remained only the Army staff car, the chauffeur, and the "bird" colonel. With no escorting motorcycles this time, and at a leisurely pace, they drove me back to the big Gray Ghost in the middle of the Clyde River. On the way back the colonel again swore me to secrecy. "No guessing, no arriving at conclusions, no repeating anything you may have heard the wounded man say, so long as you live."

All this activity in the early morning hours, and I hadn't even missed a chow call. I walked into the chow line, and a couple of my friends nodded. Only Draper asked, "Copeland, where have you been all morning?"

"Fishing," I answered.

No one else was even curious about my absence, but a couple of nights later Colonel Cohn, our Transport Surgeon, when he was making the rounds of the Main Deck wounded, stopped next to me for a moment. When I looked up he winked and gave me the "thumbs up" sign. I was sure then that he had been in on my sortie into the Third Reich, and that the patient must have survived.

But I didn't make the connection with Herman Ephrain Cohen until thirty years later. I didn't realize he was the one who had considered me a fit candidate for this very special duty. I didn't realize his opinion of me was a whole lot better than my opinion of him.

It's kind of late to offer my apologies, but I'm offering them now. Hermie, wherever you are, you sure were one helluva fine actor when it made a difference!

The kite flyer

The winds of spring blow west to east most of the time across the gently-rolling farmlands south of Cross Plains, Indiana. In those days the Stegemillers' big farm home lay a couple hundred yards west of the highway that meanders between Cross Plains and Vevay. My parents' farm was a few hundred yards east of the highway, so the distance between our two houses was less than a quarter of a mile. There were five of us boys who were fast friends: the two Stegemiller boys, their cousin, Cliff, from the little town of Rising Sun a few miles away, and my brother, Ross, and myself. We spent a lot of time together in the early spring flying kites. It was a challenge to try to make the kites fly from the Stegemiller farm over to our place, or vice versa, but we seldom got that accomplished. There was always some type of "equipment" failure, a busted string or faulty tail, or just as often, a big pin oak in the wrong place at the wrong time. But we never worried about our lack of success: we'd stash our kites, or what was left of them, and invite ourselves into Mabel Stegemiller's big kitchen which was always full of delicious smells, and especially the delicate aroma of the oatmeal cakes for which Mrs. Stegemiller was famous, which we called "coogan," a childhood distortion of the German word "kuchen."

But the good times of boyhood were a distant memory. In the intervening years we had each gone our separate ways. All of us were destined to see service in World War II. Herb Stegemiller went to Africa with the First Armored Division as a tank maintenance specialist. Mike sweated it out as a crewman on a Liberty ship in the Pacific. My brother, Ross, was with the 45th Infantry Division, and saw action in Africa, Italy and France; Cliff was with the 94th Division of the 302nd Regiment, "C" Company, in France and Germany; and I was the "bedpan commando."

In the late winter of 1945 Cliff Stegemiller's company was on duty in the Saar region when Cliff heard the telltale click of a "bouncing Betty" mine that his foot had just activated. There were two things a soldier could do when this happened: if his reactions were fast, he could freeze his foot where it was and the explosion would stay under his foot, in which case he would certainly lose the foot and perhaps the leg; or he could do the instinctive thing and jump away, in which case the mine would spring up about chest level and explode, and there wasn't much chance for his survival. Whichever Cliff did, the result was that he was badly wounded, his right leg severely damaged, his left arm, chest and abdomen riddled by shrapnel.

In late March of 1945 we unloaded our last batch of troops which would see battle in Europe, and we took on a greater-than-usual number of wounded troops. We already had hospital facilities on Main Deck and A Deck. We were so overcrowded this trip we had to utilize B Deck with its canvas racks as well, as a hospital for the late arrivals.

The beds on B deck had been stacked four tiers high, in order to get as many troops on board the ship as possible. For healthy men this was not too great an inconvenience, but for wounded soldiers it was difficult. We had quickly found that the best way to handle the situation was to place the men who were bedfast on the two highest racks and the ambulatory patients on the two bottom racks. We also found that it was less painful for a badly-wounded man, especially those encased in a body or spica cast, if one person lifted him into the rack where he would stay until we landed in New York. Since I was both tall and strong I was usually the one who did the lifting onto the high racks.

On this particular trip I was lifting a soldier up to the fourth tier when I saw that his embarkation tag had "Indiana" stencilled on it in large letters.

"Hey, I've got a Hoosier here," I exclaimed.

"Yeah, you're right," he said.

"What part?" I asked.

"Southeast part of the state, Ohio County. Betwen Aurora and Rising Sun," he explained.

I grabbed the tag then and saw his last name, "Stegemiller." I looked more closely at him. "You're not Herb . . . or Mike, either. No, I can see that. I'm from around Cross Plains myself . . ."

"Hey," I had gotten a better look at the tag, "you're Cliff, aren't you? Maybe you don't remember me. We used to fly kites together. Bob Copeland here."

We chatted for a few minutes and then I had to go help the litter bearers unload more casualties.

The C Deck swimming pool was used for troop quarters.

*D Deck tourist class staterooms were converted to house 15 men.
Crowded, yes, but still space enough for a little game.*

My regular station that trip was Main Deck, starboard side, but I made it a point to go down to B Deck to talk to Cliff at least once a day. It was on my first visit that I got to know the wounded man on the rack below his. This young soldier, whose name I have never been able to recall, could walk, which was why he had been placed on a lower bunk, but he was blind. A searing white-hot flash of high explosives had fried the corneas of the young man's eyes. The miracle was that the steel shrapnel had missed him altogether, so that in every other respect he was whole.

"I remember when we sailed from Charleston," he said in his gentle southern drawl, "how I hoped I would live through the war and return to New York so I could see the Statue of Liberty, but now that's . . ." His voice trailed off, as he fought for control.

Neither Cliff nor I could think of anything to say for a moment. Then a thought occurred to me.

"You know," I said to him, "I think we can get you two out on the Promenade Deck when we pass the Statue of Liberty as we enter the harbor. You, who can walk, and Cliff who can't walk, but can see, and me, I, who can do both, we can help each other and get you out there. How's that sound?"

It sounded good to both of them, and whenever I got to B Deck to visit with them they would bring the subject up. That particular trip was a rough one, both weather-wise and duty-wise. On Main Deck starboard we had seventy-nine patients, including six amputees, one double amputee, nineteen colostomies and fifty-three with more routine wounds.

The colostomies were the biggest problem. A colostomy is a surgical procedure in which part of the colon is removed, and a new connection is made from the remaining colon to the outside of the body, to permit evacuation. I don't know how they handle colostomy patients today, they probably have far more sophisticated techniques than we did, but what we did then was to cover the external connection with a large porous pad, which meant almost continuous diaper changing when

the Atlantic swells made those who had been shot, bayonnetted or otherwise injured in the abdominal area, seasick.

So I was on duty most of the time, but whenever I had a
minute off duty during the next couple of days and wasn't vis-
iting Cliff and my other friend on B Deck, I was in A143 trying
to write a few descriptive comments that might have meaning
to the blind soldier, to make the moment when we passed the
Statue of Liberty especially meaningful to him.

When the day shift appeared to relieve us on that morning
we were scheduled to arrive in New York, I headed for A143
and the sack, and only kicked my shoes off before I fell asleep.
As busy as we were I had momentarily forgotten my promise
to Cliff and the blind soldier, but I knew that I would need to
get up as soon as we landed to help with the debarkation. It
seemed as if I had only touched the bed when the sound of a
band playing "Sentimental Journey" penetrated my stupor.

"Oh, my God!" I thought, as I yanked on my shoes. "We're
almost up to the Statue of Liberty and those guys are waiting
for me ..." I hurried through the corridors and down to B
Deck Hospital where I was greeted by two sad faces which
brightened up quickly when I said, "OK, we still have time."

The blind man could walk, but Cliff couldn't. I carried him,
well wrapped in blankets, and the blind soldier held on to my
arm as we made our maddeningly-slow progress towards
Promenade Deck, port side, where thousands of others were
doing what we were trying to do, to see Miss Liberty as we
steamed slowly up The Narrows connecting Upper New York
Bay with Lower New York Bay.

It was mid-morning, and the sun glistening on the emerald-
green water made little sparkles of light which reflected up on
the colossal statue holding her torch aloft, causing her to appear as if she had just risen from a cooling bath in the sea. I
suddenly realized that I had never seen the statue before myself, except in photographs. I had always been busy in the hospital when we had made our passes into and out of New York
Harbor.

Suddenly, the hand holding on to my arm tightened and a voice choked with emotion begged, "Now . . . tell me . . . what . . . she looks like, please."

I am not usually at a loss for words, but this time I was. I had forgotten the two sheets of paper on which I had written the comments I intended to make. They were back in Cabin A143 in my duffel bag. But, again, I called on my memory and I tried to say them exactly as I had written them on paper, which, as nearly as I can recollect now after so many years, went something like this:

"By the grace of God, I stand here, humbly, in the company of two heroic men who have been injured while fighting for our country, and we all thrill to the beauty and the dream represented by that shining statue only a quarter of a mile away on Bedloe's Island given to us by the people of France. She wears a crown and she carries a torch aloft in her upraised hand, and stands, by my guess, about 300 feet tall. But not so tall as you two stand as you return to the country you have fought for so ably. This will not be the last time liberty will have to be defended, and men like you will need to pass on your courage to others."

And then I tried to describe how the sun glistened on the green-tinted copper statue, and how she appeared to me. I went on to recite the words at the base which I had learned by heart as a schoolboy many years earlier: "Give me your tired, your poor, your huddled masses yearning to breathe free . . ."

One can't shed tears when the tear ducts have become burned scars, so our blinded comrade only sobbed and nodded his thanks. But Cliff and I shed a few.

Cliff was sent to Halloran General Hospital in New York City. I left the *Queen* at 9:00 o'clock the next morning, after all the wounded troops had disembarked and, with some good fortune in picking up rides, was able to knock on Mrs. Stegemiller's door in Aurora, Indiana at 11:00 o'clock that evening. I don't blame the two ladies, mother and daughter-in-law, for being hesitant about opening the door to a uniformed stranger at that hour of the night, but they were up, anyway, giving a

"We made our maddeningly-slow progress towards Promenade Deck, port side, where thousands of others were doing what we were trying to do."

"...I tried to describe how the sun glistened on the green-tinted copper statue..."

Pier 90, always a welcome sight.

baby its bottle. I told them quickly who I was, how I had happened to see Cliff, and why Cliff had asked me to stop by to tell them that he had arrived in New York. I told them that Cliff was in the hospital but was going to be all right, that he sent his love, and would be happy to hear that he was the father of a son or daughter. I had a good Samaritan waiting for me in his car, with motor running, to drive me home, so I had to wait thirty-six years to find out that the baby, a strapping 7-1/2 pounder, was a girl.

Isadore Weinstein, soldier

It was a hot day in July, 1945 that I was awakened by reveille as usual, not knowing that this day would be unique, because this was the day I would meet Isadore Weinstein (pseudonym).

A small contingent entered through the inward-swinging door to the hospital, three tough-looking combat troops, followed by Isadore Weinstein.

Let me describe Isadore. In the first place, I was considered tall in those days: I usually towered over most of my friends. But next to Isadore, I looked downright puny. Isadore was at least six foot seven, and weighed about 280 pounds. He had black curly hair and a red handlebar moustache, which was waxed and curled up at the ends. Add to this enormous pop-eyes (probably exophthalmia caused by a thyroid imbalance), extra-large hands and feet and long arms, and you had a sensation of raw power in an ungainly package. He was wearing combat boots and grenade hooks.

His buddies had brought him in for an infected thumb. Men were returning from battle via the "happy route," Camp Lucky Strike or Camp Home Run (both in France), and then across the Channel to a "health resort" called Tidworth Staging Area.

Tidworth was not a true military camp, but a collection of shelters set up for staging the invasion of Europe. The most charitable thing I ever heard said about Tidworth was that it was bearable, if you were leaving the next day; otherwise there were seven places in hell that were more comfortable. Fortunately, stays at Tidworth were routinely short, and lasted only until you were assigned to a homeward-bound ship. But troops were being sent home in large numbers at this time, and the available ships were in short supply, so it was not always as short a stay at Tidworth as the primitive accommodations would warrant.

The barracks were unheated, and it was unseasonably damp and chilly. Isadore had taken an axe and gone out to chop up some kindling for a bonfire when the axe slipped and smashed his left thumbnail. Tidworth apparently did not have extensive medical facilities, so nothing had been done about it. By the time I saw him the whole thumb had become badly infected under the nail, and there was danger of gangrene setting in.

While Major Freund was examining Isadore's thumb, I had an enlightening discussion with his two buddies.

Isadore was an American Jew of German stock. He hated all Nazis, and with good reason, because fourteen of his close relatives had died in concentration camps. The men said Isadore had sworn to avenge his relatives, and that he had a small piece of cardboard in his wallet with each of the fourteen names listed. He drew a line through a name on the list each time he killed an enemy soldier. One of the men said he had glimpsed the now bloodsmeared list, and that nearly all the names were lined out.

Major Freund determined that Isadore's whole nail would have to come off, and he asked me to do the job while he tended other patients. Isadore followed me into the operating room, and I began preparing a hypodermic syringe to shoot some pain-deadening novocaine into the thumb.

"No one sticks me with a needle!" His deep voice was as awe-inspiring as his appearance.

I explained, in my most professional manner, that the pain would be excruciating if the thumb were not deadened first.

"You cut out the thumbnail, I'll handle the pain. But no needle."

"OK, soldier," I said, "but I don't want to have a botched-up job if you flinch."

But he didn't flinch. He never moved, he never twitched. I would have sworn his eyelashes never came down once over those bug eyes of his, but I couldn't be sure because I was busy doing my job. I saw him a couple more times before we got to New York, but I always got a cold chill when I looked at him. I thanked God I hadn't been an enemy soldier across the hedgerow from Isadore Weinstein. And I often wondered if the cardboard list had been completely lined through, or if not, if he had taken his vengeance against any of the Germans who immigrated to this country after the war. I wondered if this man ever found a way to exorcize his hate. I wondered if he ever had a family and children, and what he taught them about the war. I wonder if he ever made peace with his fellow men.

Henri

Sometime, somewhere in the hellish wreckage that was Belgium in the fall of 1944, some men of one of the Airborne divisions, I think it was the 82nd, rescued a pint-sized old man of eleven or twelve years who was one of the many personal tragedies of the war. He had lost not only his home, his family, and all his friends and relations, but also his childhood.

Henri attached himself to whatever outfit it was and followed them through the snowy meat-grinder of the Ardennes and Hurtgen Forest and all the other locations where General Runstedt and his Wehrmacht chose to fight in that last hurrah of the conflict in Europe that we later came to refer to as the "Battle of the Bulge." Legend has it that Henri's surrogate "mothers" used a couple of cartons of cigarettes to bribe someone handy with a needle to cut down and tailor a uniform for him; however acquired, he looked exactly like a paratrooper, in miniature, and he tried to act like one, too. Henri was too small to handle one of their guns, but he became deadly accurate with hand grenades.

The problem, of course, was what to do with Henri when the unit was scheduled to return to the States. His buddies solved it by smuggling him aboard the *Q.M.* in a duffel bag, but a steward caught on to them as they were letting him out of the bag after the ship had sailed, and he was immediately declared a stowaway.

The Chief Steward of the *Queen Mary*, who stood second only to God in the Cunard ship hierarchy, appeared in the hospital the morning of our sailing, visibly in pain when he walked, and obviously distressed in spirit. This august personage had been introduced to Henri, and had suffered a well-placed kick in the shin instead of the more orthodox handshake, and a string of American profanity quite beyond his comprehension instead of a courteous response to an introduction.

The Chief hemmed and hawed a bit, and I asked if I couldn't put something soothing on his injured shinbone. It was while I was tending his leg that he came to the point.

"You see, Sergeant Copeland, this is a rawther delicate matter. It seems this little bugger has considerable backing from his companions, and I am afraid I will precipitate a war between two of the Allies if I order Henri to the brig, which is of course what I should do."

I agreed with the Chief that he did, indeed, have a problem. Then he suggested, rather diffidently, but much as though he were offering me Piccadilly Circus in London for $10 and a chance on a set of dishes, that I could solve his dilemma by allowing him to parole Henri to my custody until we made land.

Now it never hurts one bit to stay on good terms with a Chief Steward, so I said I'd do it.

"Good show," said the Chief and departed anon, *his* problem having now become *my* problem.

Henri was immediately delivered to me, but I not only now had Henri to look after, I also had his armed guard to take into account, when four non-coms from the Division showed up simultaneously, regarding me with open hostility. The message was plain, and being no fool myself, between us GI's a bargain was thereupon struck: since the Chief Steward had not set any ground rules, I allowed as how I would keep Henri with me during the day; I would treat him as if he were my own son and heir, feed him, wash him, and provide suitable entertainment; and that I would return him to his boon companions in the evenings when the lights were low and no one would be the wiser. Everyone seemed satisfied with this arrangement except the subject himself, who called me a "sone-um-a-beetch" and took his vengeance upon my shins as well.

But gradually Henri accepted the situation. In fact, he had the best of both worlds. I fed him hospital grub, and gave him comic books, took him down to "those guys" in the troop quarters at night, and got up a little early each morning to pick up the sleeping boy and carry him back to the hospital. Henri became less aggressive, but he still had his favorite adjective which he used whenever he addressed me: over and over he would preface son-of-a-bitch with a word I didn't know—it sounded like "foomeedobble."

One night when I sneaked Henri back down to those men he loved, I asked them what he was saying, and he happily responded by once more calling me a "foomeedobble sone-um-a-beetch." One of his "mothers" in GI battle harness laughed and said, "Sarge, that's French. It's spelled f-o-r-m-i-d-a-b-l-e, and it means exactly what our English word means, that you are big, tough, overbearing."

Overbearing? No, sir. No medic with any desire for survival would think of being overbearing to a little soldier whose bosom companions were so numerous and so formidable themselves.

Gradually, Henri came to trust me. Before we got to New York he even allowed me to look at his shrapnel scars and put a little salve on those angry red blotches. He still called me a son-of-a-bitch a few times each day, but I felt it was because he had come to like me, too.

The last time I saw Henri an Army officer in New York had him in tow and Henri was giving him the verbal baptism of fire. Rumor had it they were going to deport him back to Belgium where he had nothing to return to. I know one of "those guys," a fatherly-looking sergeant, had told me he and his wife wanted to adopt Henri. But whether the powers that be, or were, in the military and immigration service, vetoed this sensible, compassionate solution I was never to learn.

I wish I did know what happened to the little fellow.

Jastrow

Jastrow (pseudonym) was a paratrooper who had drawn duty as a Pier Guard, and was sometimes assigned to guard the *Q.M.* when she was tied up at Pier 90. The first time we met him he let us know how unhappy he was with the Army. He had 169 points towards discharge at a time when it only took 90 to be sent back to civilian life, unless you were, like me, frozen in place because of special needs. Certainly pier guard duty wasn't special duty of a high order, and I didn't understand why Jastrow wasn't scheduled for discharge.

I didn't understand, that is, until my friend who was the real honcho of the pier guards let me peek at his record, and then I understood. And it no longer seemed strange that he didn't carry a pistol as the other guards did, only a much-shortened version of a billy-club.

I told my roommates in A143 what I had glimpsed in Jastrow's record, and that's how we came to let him sit in our one chair every time he came to visit A143, which turned out to be every time he drew *Queen Mary* guard duty.

The British called our paratroopers "the wild men." A German officer found dead in a battle with the 82nd Airborne had written his last entry in a personal diary in which he said he felt death was imminent at the hands of "those devils in baggy pants." Their reputation as fighting men was well-deserved, and our Jastrow, the one to whom we always gave our chair, was prominent among them.

Tough and wiry of stature, his service record showed personal bravery almost beyond imagining. The Airborne gave out no medals for ordinary heroism; and the recipient of medals in that outfit was, more often than not, dead when the award was made.

Jastrow was the exception. I remember seeing a Silver Star listed on his record, perhaps two, and several Purple Hearts, which were awarded for injuries occurring at different times in different battles prior to the last one he was engaged in; but I took special note there was no mention of any hospitalizations until after the jump into Holland.

I should begin by giving Jastrow's own account of the last few hours at the staging area in the Midlands of England where the Airborne had re-grouped and re-armed and re-trained. There were many new faces since the first battles in Sicily and Italy which had taken such a heavy toll, new faces and a new problem. Everyone in the European theater at that time knew what a hot item the sleek paratrooper boots had become. Ordinary soldiers, and even civilians, who knew somebody in the supply rooms or the Quartermaster Corps were showing up wearing them. Consequently, they were in short supply and it was becoming harder and harder for the paratroopers themselves, the men of the 82nd and the 101st, for whom they were a necessary item of equipment, to get boots of the correct size issued to them.

The thought of jumping behind enemy lines in the dark with 100 pounds of ammo, weapons, and rations strapped to their backs, and depending on regular combat shoes to sustain the legs and ankles, was a real worry to those "wild men." There at the staging area, in the English Midlands, restricted to camp and only hours until the historic jump into Holland, Jastrow had only combat shoes to wear. He knew the facts of life for a paratrooper: break an ankle on the way in and you're a dead paratrooper.

He sat there in our only chair in A143 while we listened.

And the room was hushed as he continued his story.

Breaking restriction he went over the fence and into town looking for someone wearing his size of paratrooper boots. After much searching he found a likely candidate for exchanging footwear. The only trouble was, the other guy, a soldier, not a paratrooper, told Jastrow, nothing doing! Jastrow gave him ten seconds to start unlacing, and when the soldier gave him the finger and started to walk away, Jastrow pulled out his .45 and shot him.

"I never in my life heard so many whistles blowin', so many people screamin'. It's a hell of a job to keep wavin' a pistol and unlace boots from someone else's feet at the same time," Jastrow explained.

He made it, though, and he also made it back over the fence where everything was ready for boarding the planes and gliders. The restricted camp and the rush of last-minute preparations kept his crime a secret from the military authorities until after his unit had taken off in the planes headed for Holland.

Books have been written about what happened that night when the "devils in baggy pants" made their landing in the low country. Hundreds died when gliders crashed or Nazi guns found the mark below a swaying parachute. Jastrow was one of the ones who made it to the ground in good condition. Then he had to watch helplessly as one of his close friends got caught in the branches of a nearby tree and was butchered—the enemy knifed you in the belly or bayonetted you as you struggled to free yourself from the shrouds of a parachute caught in the tree limbs.

Jastrow's own account, matter of factly related, matched exactly with what the Pier Sergeant showed me later in his record after I got to wondering whether Jastrow was exaggerating a bit.

Recorded: 27 enemy soldiers killed . . . 7 separate wounds . . . 1 tank destroyed . . . still alive when medics were able to get him down from the tree where he had taken refuge for his last stand . . . 6 wounds when he climbed up the tree overhanging the road . . . 1 grenade left . . . near nighfall, a lone Nazi tank clanking, around the bend in the road, unbuttoned . . . last grenade dropped down the hatch as the tank passed under the tree ... 7th wound *of the day* from shapnel out of the open hatch ...

Another Silver Star, and then the inevitable. The killing of the soldier back in England, in order to get the boots, caught up with him in a field hospital. He was up for general court martial on a charge of murder. The record was vague as to what happened next, but Jastrow filled us in.

"Hell's fire, the whole outfit told 'em if they court-martialled me, they'd have to fight all the 82nd and 101st, so it was sort of dropped."

Sort of dropped, but they wouldn't discharge him. Jastrow said he could hardly wait until he and his brother got home so he could straighten out the brother who, in a letter home from the Pacific, had stated his opinion that the marines were tougher than the paratroopers. The paratroopers only "smelled" tough, he told Mom Jastrow, and Mom Jastrow made the mistake of passing on this bit of braggadocio from her son, the Marine, to her son, the Paratrooper.

But all this explained the lack of a pistol, the shortened billy-club and the failure to discharge Jastrow, when he had enough points to get two men out of the Army.

The last time I saw Jastrow I was down near the aft gangplank at Pier 90, when a big contingent of men from the 8th Air Force were coming off the ship. I was loading the hospital's soiled laundry onto a truck when I heard loud, angry voices. I turned around and observed some horseplay going on up inside the ship disrupting the orderly check-off of each man as he disembarked.

Jastrow was there at the foot of the gangplank, telling the men to stay in their lines so they could be checked off.

Then one of the guys who was making the disturbance, an 8th Air Force sergeant at least as tall and heavy as I was, made one of the biggest mistakes of his military career. He taunted Jastrow, calling him a "rear-echelon bastard."

Jastrow yelled, "I'll rear-echelon you!" and with that he threw his diminutive billy club out into the water between the ship and the pier and climbed the outside of the gangplank like a monkey until he reached the doorway where the name-calling sergeant was standing. Jastrow hung on to the rail of the gangplank with his left hand and swung his right fist hard at the sergeant's face. The sergeant's duffel bag landed with a splash in the Hudson River, and the sergeant himself fell backwards, taking down a couple of men in the crowd behind him. Jastrow was on top of him like an avenging animal, yelling and rubbing the sergeant's face with a handful of something he had pulled out of his pocket.

I thought I'd never get up there through the crowd of men and baggage. It took three of us to pull Jastrow off the prostrate sergeant, and then I saw what Jastrow had used to scratch the sergeant's face so badly. His campaign ribbons with battle stars . . . his decorations for bravery . . . his purple hearts with clusters. All of Jastrow's decorations and medals were banded together on clips intended to be worn on the left chest of military uniforms. It was, of course, the weapon most suited to the insult . . .

Men from Pier Guard headquarters there on Pier 90 arrived and took Jastrow away. Very gently. Very courteously. With some help, I assisted the injured airman to the hospital and reopened the operating room to do some first aid, and then sent him on to Halloran General nearby for more extensive treatment. I was angry with him, so not much conversation passed between us, but finally he asked a question.

"Was that son-of-a-bitch really authorized to have all that fruit salad he nailed me with?"

I should have given the sergeant a full account of Jastrow's service record, to teach him a little humility. Instead, all I said was:

"You bet your life he was!"

Piv

Raymond West was a friend of my younger brother. When I left home he was a skinny, tow-headed little fellow who had trouble articulating certain sounds. I remember one day he announced he was going to play basketball when he grew up, and was going to be the "pivot man" on the team, only he pronounced it "pivvy man." Thereafter we all began calling him "Pivvy," which as he grew older was shortened to "Piv," and I suppose most people forgot how he had ever gotten the nickname in the first place.

I hadn't seen Ray for nine years, but in one of her letters my mother told me that Ray was a paratrooper with the 82nd Airborne, and I should watch out for him. Since the 82nd had already hit Europe it was unlikely he would travel back with us unless he had bad luck and got wounded. I did check the list of wounded from time to time, just in case.

The war in the European Theater ended May 6, 1945, but it was several months before they began sending some of the combat divisions home. My first intimation that these combat divisions would be traveling with us on our next trip to New York came when I ran into a fellow from the 82nd Airborne in London right after Christmas. Al Draper and I were walking near Piccadilly Circus one foggy evening when we were accosted by a brash young "devil in baggy pants." He had a female companion on each arm, and asked if he could buy that bottle of hooch from me. I denied I had any such commodity. He said, "I mean the one with the neck sticking out of your raincoat!"

Sure enough, the neck of a bottle of Southern Comfort was sticking out of the pocket of my raincoat. I thought I had it carefully hidden, but somehow it had pushed its way up, probably when I transferred the coat from one arm to another.

"Not for sale," I said. Al and I had brought the whiskey as a gift for Nicholas Brodsky, Alex Paal, and our other Hungarian friends. However, this prospective purchaser was insistent, and he was loaded with cash. When the offer got as high as $25.00 Al decided friendship was one thing and commerce another. We made the exchange. I gave the paratrooper some fatherly advice. I told him to be careful because Southern Comfort packed quite a wallop, and he looked amused. Thanks anyway, dad, but he'd been around, and he was going to have one helluva last fling before his outfit left for the States in two days.

"You'll be sailing with us then," I said, "maybe we'll see you on the ship."

"Yeah, mebbee," he said, not much convinced that our paths would ever cross again. And yet, as a matter of fact, they did: several days out on the westbound journey after Amkraut had pronounced a laboratory slide positive, I had to give Friend Paratrooper the standard 100,000 units of penicillin to send him home clean and whole.

It was the last time the *Queen* was to return with a full-strength complement of troops. We had both the 82nd and the 101st Airbornes, commanded by General Jim Gavin, at thirty-seven the youngest major general in the history of our Army. Both these units were mostly replacements, not the grizzled veterans you'd expect, but they looked like fighting men, and they were fighting men. There was an aura of pride about them, and a sense of comradeship. As soon as they embarked they posted their own guards, and their guards carried M-1 rifles. That was the first and only time during my tenure on the *Queen* that guards posted around the ship to watch out for fires or other untoward events, carried loaded weapons.

The paratroopers were also subject to intense discipline, even on the trip home, and they insisted on having the use of the ship's brig, which they soon had full of unlucky devils guilty of what we considered innocuous offenses, an indiscreet smoke on deck, for example. We thought we ran a tight ship, but those fellows made us look like Girl Scouts on retreat.

Meantime, every chance I had I went to look at the passenger list to see if I could find Raymond West's name. When I finally did, I went down into the troop section where he was supposed to be, and called out "Raymond West, Raymond West" as loud as I could. No one answered, and no one admitted to knowing him. I went again the next morning, again with the same negative result. Then at chow that day Bill Roush had a suggestion: "Why don't you take off the PS armband?"

he said. ("P.S." stood for "permanent staff.") "Maybe he thinks you're trying to get him on a work detail."

So I peeled off the armband and went down to the troop quarters and tried again. Nothing. Then I had a brilliant idea. I remembered suddenly his nickname of long ago.

"Pivvy," I shouted, "you louse-bound Hoosier from Cross Plains, Indiana, answer me!"

A tall, well-built man in full paratrooper regalia started uncoiling from the rack almost at my knees. He had an incredulous look on his face.

"Bob Copeland, is that you?"

I grabbed him and gave him a friendly shake. He had been lying low thinking, as Bill Roush had guessed, that he was wanted for some sort of work detail. From then on we were able to spend time together in the evenings when I snuck him into the petty officers' mess with us, and later walked him back to A143 where we spent hours rapping about old times and old friends, and he recounted some of his experiences as a paratrooper for the benefit of me and my roommates.

Piv had sailed to England on our *Queen* unbeknownst to me, of course, and arrived at the Midlands in England where he had joined up with his unit as they prepared for the assault on the Continent. He had been injured in the Battle of the Bulge, and was still recuperating when the jump beyond the Rhine River took place, but he was allowed to drive a truck across the river, loaded with ammo and food. The Airborne was nearing the Elbe, pushing towards Berlin when the command decision was made to "Hold up" so the Russians could enter Berlin before the rest of the Allied Forces—a decision we have never ceased to regret.

And Piv? What happened to him? Now he drives an 18-wheeler for Roadway Express out of the Cincinnati Terminal, and probably none of his fellow truckers or the dispatchers on his regular run between Buffalo and Cincinnati realize that this friendly "Big R" driver with the ingratiating smile was once one of those "devils in baggy pants" who, when the annals of World War II are written, count as the bravest of the brave.

The mess line.

The gang at the Palace of Versailles.

Chapter 7

THE END OF HOSTILITIES

V-E Day

It was obvious when we sailed from the Clyde Anchorage on the 30th of April, 1945 that the end of the war in Europe was imminent. When we arrived in New York it was even more apparent, because the *Queen Elizabeth* had been docked for several days at Pier 90 waiting for a decision to be made about the future of both of the big ships. When news of the surrender came we were restricted to ship, I suppose because we might be required to sail without much notice. We weren't too happy about that, but there was one redeeming factor to our confinement. The English have a pleasant maritime ritual called "splicing the main brace." If an occasion of national rejoicing is declared by the British sovereign all ships flying under the flag of Britain or any of her dominions will issue a "tot of rum" to all hands. Those of us who were more or less permanent fixtures on the *Queen* were included in the festivities by the old timers, and we appreciated the favor shown us—we also appreciated the tot of rum.

Security around the Gray Ghost and her sister ship for some reason was even tighter than usual during this period. The temporary glut of big ships in New York harbor overtaxed the MP detachment quartered on the upper level of Pier 90, so when security was strengthened some of us who were restricted to ship but unassigned, were pressed into service. Four consecutive nights I drew twelve-hour guard duty in the engine rooms, two nights in our ship and two nights on the *Queen Elizabeth*. I was friends with the MP sergeant in charge of posting the guards so he took me along when he was giving assignments to other men. We kept going down, deck after deck, until finally we were in the aft underbelly of the ship where the engine room is located. I was almost overcome by the putrid stench from the nearby bilges, and I could understand then why the area is referred to as the "bowels" of a ship. I also understood at that moment why the sergeant had that extra pistol belt slung over his shoulder.

"I'm a medic, Sarge, in case you didn't know."

"I didn't hear that," he said.

"Hey, but I've never shot a .45."

"I didn't hear that either," he snapped.

"Okay, if that's the way it's got to be, show me how the damn thing works." Some friend you turned out to be, I thought to myself.

"All right, this here is the safety. Push it this way and you're ready for business." He pushed the safety on and off. "It's got a full clip, and here are three spare clips. Stick 'em in your pocket."

"What are the orders?" I asked.

"Anyone shows up here and in a damn few seconds doesn't convince you he has business here, you draw the gun, understand?" he growled.

"And then what?"

"Quit askin' so many damn fool questions. You're gonna have to decide. We can't let the engine room be sabotaged. Do whatever you have to do."

He left, and like any ten year-old kid I took the .45 out of its holster and removing the clip, kept moving the safety back and forth, simulating the action of firing. On the one hand I was thrilled with the idea I might have to defend my ship, be a real soldier. On the other hand I was remembering some stories I had heard. The 160,000 horsepower plants of the *Queen Mary* and the *Queen Elizabeth* are impressive sights. Crewmen had told me about one time when superheated steam from one of them had just simply drilled a hole through a pipefitter who was trying to repair a tiny leak. I had a healthy respect for the area I was guarding.

But nothing happened. I was not destined to become a hero; and the only injury to my body was to my sense of smell, from which I recovered quickly.

Paris, the first time

I always thought it was a pretty song, the one that went "The last time I saw Paris, her heart was warm and gay . . ."

But when I saw Paris the first time she wasn't warm and she wasn't gay. Her people were cold and hungry and not gay at all.

To a nine year-old boy from Cross Plains, Indiana, who spent his free spring and summer days plowing his daddy's fields with a team of three horses hitched to a walking plow, a Saturday afternoon trip to Versailles, Indiana (pronounced "ver-sales") nine miles away was a big-time adventure. It was inconceivable that he would grow up to see the European city for which it was named, Versailles, France (pronounced "vair-sigh"). But he did.

It was in the late fall of 1945, after the *Queen* had gone home again to her Southampton docks, when the announcement was made over the intercom that U.S. Army Staff personnel would be permitted to take a 72-hour trip to the Continent if they so desired—at their own expense, of course.

For most of my buddies that last clause constituted no problem. They knew that such things could be financed by means of the much sought-after American cigarette. Me, dummy that I was, because I didn't smoke, I had been passing up the free

Red Cross cartons given us each trip, and now was berating myself for my lack of financial foresight. Fortunately, the musketeer's philosophy was alive and well in our unit: the medics I travelled with came up with about six cartons and I shared equally with the others in the community pot.

We managed to hitch a ride on the *Marshal Joffre* which was ready to depart for LeHavre with troops that had only hours before been travelling with us. Parenthetically, and paradoxically, after twenty crossings of the unpredictable and ofttimes surly Atlantic with nary a lost meal or uncomfortable moment, in sailing over this little inch and a half on the map between Southampton and LeHavre, in a becalmed sea, I had my first bout with sea sickness.

The wreckage we saw at LeHavre was worse than anything we could have imagined. Before D-Day the Allied Command had noted the huge build-up of armament and ships in LeHavre and decided it was vital to the invasion to wipe it out. For many hours, planes dropped thousands of leaflets, printed in French, all over the city, warning everyone that a destructive bombing was about to take place and that people should evacuate to avoid injury or death. Naturally, many persons ignored the warnings, and many French civilians died. For thirty-six hours our 8th Air Force and the British Air Force, in a joint operation, relentlessly targeted the harbor, and we witnessed the results. Three square miles of the dock area were totally wiped out. The masts of a hundred ships showed above the water's surface. Fragments of concrete were visible along the beach with the chilling words, **"Verboten Minen,"** painted in large black letters, and piles of rubble in a sort of path were all that remained of the service road.

But war has its comical side, too. As the group of us were gathered on the deck above the gangplank waiting for the troops to debark, our attention was caught by two U.S. sailors walking along the shore with an ever-increasing crowd of French men, women, and children following in their wake, diving every now and then to the ground, in a wild scramble of legs and arms and bashing heads. Our eagle-eyed corporal,

Otto Wrablik, let us know what was happening: "They're losin' cigarettes out from under their bell bottoms!" he said.

To compound the sailors' misery, a U.S. Navy Shore Patrol was approaching from the opposite direction. What they saw was at least twenty cigarette-hungry Frenchmen mobbing two sailors for contraband cigarettes which the enterprising sailors had stored inside the legs of over-sized knee-length socks. The socks gave way under the weight, and the packs began falling out, one at a time. I don't know what the shore patrol did to the two unlucky gobs, but an educated guess is that they took the two miscreants back to their ship, confiscated the remaining packs, and then divvied up the contraband among themselves. And I would lay odds on that.

After we finally were allowed to leave the ship and were waiting for the train to Paris, we walked through the wreckage to a military staging area which had been whimsically titled "Camp Home Run." We were sitting at a couple of tables drinking some good, hot, strong coffee, when I realized that I was getting overtly hostile looks from French civilians working behind the counter. Several minutes later an MP came over and sat down with us. After some desultory small talk he turned and asked me if I intended to wear the cap I had on my head whileI was in France.

I was truly puzzled.

"It's a regulation Army garrison cap," I said.

"Mac, it may be that to you and me, but to these Frenchies it's an Air Force cap. They don't feel anything but hate for the Air Force, either ours or the British, and you'll more likely stay healthy if you don't wear it while you're in France."

After this explanation I hastily beat a path to the supply office at the camp and pleaded my case to the supply sergeant. After some haggling I departed with just a plain "overseas" cap, and regretfully left my more stylish garrison cap with him. He got the better of that bargain, but my visit to France was unmarred by any more outward displays of animosity towards my person, so it was a good deal for me, too.

Eventually the train came in and we boarded, and were glad to be at last going somewhere. We did go somewhere: thirty miles, at least. Then the train slowed down gradually until it finally stopped, and then, after a minute or two, started rolling gently backwards.

"I guess we're going back to pick up some VIP who missed the train at LeHavre," Draper joked.

But I didn't laugh. It seemed strange that we had come to a stop without my feeling any brake application. I had been a street car motorman for several years, and I knew something was amiss. Finally, we were enlightened by a Frenchman who stuck his head out of a window and excitedly described our predicament in fractured English.

Our group had settled in the third car from the rear of the train. Now instead of numerous cars ahead of us, and an engine, we were four cars and no engine. Somehow the cars had become uncoupled, and that explained why we had stopped and were rolling slowly backwards. Apparently no safety devices were working on the cars, but we had finally hit a "cut" where the tracks were below ground level and the cars had stopped sliding backwards. I looked out and saw bomb holes all around punctuated with torn pieces of train wheels, crossties, rails and miscellaneous junk, and wondered why we hadn't derailed.

I began shouting advice to everyone for evacuating the cars, and was the first to set a good example. When I turned and discovered no one had followed me, I saw that all my buddies were still comfortably ensconced in the train, watching me through the windows and hee-hawing.

"Come on back, Cope," Al Draper said, with mock reassurance. "The war's been over since May."

Well, I had to do something to cover my embarrassment, so I climbed the "cut" and found that it bisected a small farm. I saw a farmer plowing a field, but he was using the strangest kind of plow imaginable and a milk cow for motive power. The plow made a furrow across the field, and when the man got to the end of the row he would flip the plow upside down and come right back. This Ripley County farm boy was amazed, and I tried to talk to him when he got back to my end of the field. I didn't speak French and he didn't speak English, but he seemed to be explaining that the Nazis had conscripted his horse which was the reason he was using a cow; and I was trying to explain what had happened to the train. I think we both agreed that this was a heck of a way to plow a field or run a railroad.

It was after sunset when the front part of the train came backing down from the direction of Paris and coupled our cars in the customary manner, and quite late when the train pulled into the Gare du Nord. We hadn't had anything to eat except K-rations and that good French coffee since leaving Southampton eighteen hours earlier, so it was doubly exciting when we piled out of the station into the near-total darkness of Paris and smelled meat cooking. I was working on my second delicious "hot dog', a tube steak between two pieces of savory French bread, when an American GI stopped and looked at us in disgust.

"Do you guys really eat that stuff?" he asked.

"Man, this is really wonderful. Try one."

"Tastes better than anything I've had since I left California."

"Best hot dog I ever ate."

"Hell, it's horse meat!" he replied disdainfully, and disappeared into the darkness again.

We finished the hot dogs, but no one ordered any more. To the starving victims of war it must have seemed manna from heaven, but to those of us who had fond memories of pet ponies, or who were conditioned by American attitudes that horse meat was only meant for glue or dog food, it was not inherently edible, and what had minutes before seemed so delicious now became distasteful. So does the mind control our appetites.

At the station we had talked to a Red Cross worker who told us we could put up for the night at the Hotel Ambassador, which was being operated on an interim basis by the Red

Cross. The hotel was located in central Paris on the beautiful
Boulevard Haussmann, and provided real beds and two meals
daily for a modest charge. The food available to Parisians at
the time was limited, but we discovered that a real French cook
can do incredible magic with the simplest ingredients.

The beverages were another matter. In true French fashion
we were served coffee at breakfast and wine at lunch, but at
dinner each evening the hotel provided a beverage which I
learned was called "Benedictine." It was served in metal cups,
and with my first sip on our first evening I felt a fire traveling
down my throat into my stomach and intestines. There were
eight of us at the table, and I noticed several of the others who
had sampled the drink were surreptitiously blowing their
noses or wiping their eyes, but one hardy fellow, wearing a
combat infantryman badge, neatly drained his cup and smiled
and sighed with evident satisfaction.

He saw me coughing and sputtering.

"Don't you like it?" he asked.

I would have answered him if I could have spoken at that
point, but since my eyes were watering, my ears were ringing,
and my whole system was in turmoil, I merely shook my head
and pushed the unfinished cup in his direction. Down the
hatch it went, and almost immediately he became the recipient
of six more "iron maidens" from six other incapacitated
medics.

"Glad to help you boys out," the intrepid infantryman
laughed, as he downed his last cup.

"OK," one of us said, "but just don't light any cigarettes until some of the gasoline evaporates from your insides. We're on
leave, and we're not going to patch up any explosion victims
today."

Paris, through some international ground rules of war, had
been declared an "open" city. It was surely nice to be where
there was no wreckage. Parisians had gone through hard times,
with the long occupation by the Nazis, and even then, months
after V-E Day, food was still terribly scarce, fuel almost non-
existent, and acts of vengeance and retribution were a daily

happenstance. We saw many bald women, whose heads had been shorn as a visible means of condemnation for what their neighbors considered to be treasonable fraternizing with the enemy; and several of our group witnessed the assassination of a civilian a few blocks away from our hotel the first morning we were there.

We were walking down Boulevard Haussmann, which was bustling with pedestrians, on our way to join the tour group which was going to the palace of Versailles, when suddenly people began to flee in all directions from a lone man who himself began running up the steps of a nearby building, in hopes of shelter. He never made it. A gunman, dressed like thousands of other Frenchman on that avenue, fired three shots rapidly and disappeared into the fleeing crowd himself. Instinctively, I suppose because of being a medic, I headed towards the victim to give aid, but I didn't get far before two ordinary-looking fellows gently grabbed my arms and turned me around the other way. No words passed, but I got the message. The gendarme directing traffic from a nearby raised platform seemed not to notice anything out of the ordinary, and my friends and I walked on. I was told later this was a common way of dealing with traitors in the immediate aftermath of war.

In certain areas of Paris provision is made for gentlemen who feel the call of nature to relieve themselves without detouring from the street. There are, or were then, sheet-metal enclosures where one could walk inside and, with only the bottom of one's legs visible to passers-by, urinate into a depression in the pavement. Near one of these comfort stations situated in the vicinity of the Eiffel Tower, we met François, a most enterprising young man, and a fellow I feel sure must today run a large French corporation with considerable flair.

I should explain that a rivulet of water from a nearby hydrant served to dilute and carry the urine from these sidewalk facilities downhill to a small sewer opening, and it was at this point where the urine-laced water disappeared into the sewer that François sat and carried on his business, which waxed and waned depending on the number of those fellows seeking relief who were smokers and discarded the unused ends of their cigarettes into the flowing stream.

There sat François that chilly afternoon, retrieving soggy cigarette butts before they disappeared down the sewer. His supplies included sheets from yesterday's Paris newspaper, *Le Soir,* and his workbench was the curbstone. Deftly, he would pick up the butts, peel the paper away, and place the sodden shreds of tobacco on the newspaper to dry. No investment, no overhead, and an unending supply of raw material. We asked about that other requirement for a successful business, the customer, and François assured us that there was no dearth of buyers for the end product. It was a formula for success Henry Ford himself couldn't have improved on, and the buddy I was with, Al Draper, took note, I guess, because he now owns half of Anniston, Alabama.

Me, I'm still looking for the floating cigarette butts.

When we were at the Eiffel Tower a friendly old Frenchman pointed to tire marks on the macadam surface under the arch where one of our B17 Flying Fortresses had made a daredevil joy-pass under the tower on V-E Day as a triumphant, full-throttle salute to the end of the war in Europe; and on our way back from Versailles we detoured past what was left of Orly Airport, which then looked something like Kroot & Sons junkyard back home in Indianapolis. The difference was that Kroot's junk wasn't remnants of Stukas, Messerschmitts, Heinkels, flak towers, staff cars, tanks and army trucks. And Kroot's junk wasn't all marked with the hideous swastika which decorated Orly's junk.

Piccadilly Commando

On the afternoon of August 31, 1945 the *Queen* was docked at her home port of Southampton, and 10,000 or so troops had disembarked en route to Germany to take up occupation duty. The BBC had been continually broadcasting accounts of the impending surrender of Japan to General MacArthur. And then towards nightfall a newscaster pronounced the unconditional surrender of Japan as a fact, and excitement fed on itself. The BBC predicted that a million people would participate in a V-J celebration in London that night.

Sergeant Dean Reilly, major domo of our isolation hospital, and I, quickly closed down our establishment and took a cab to Southampton Central railway station. The train was jampacked with people doing the same thing we were, heading for London.

Near Basingbroke the engineer started to sound the train's whistle, and he never let up between there and Victoria Station.

In London we had no choice but to drift with the tide of humanity that filled the streets, which took us eventually to the focal point of most London events, Piccadilly Circus.

And circus it was. Bands of musicians were playing "Roll out the Barrel," "Lily of Piccadilly," "Waltzin' Matilda," and other patriotic or popular songs. Snake dances formed with thousands of participants serpentining back and forth in long, long lines, some of them several bodies wide, extending down the streets which intersected with Piccadilly and wrapping around corners into other streets.

Reilly and I, taking advantage of each movement of the crowd, kept edging closer to the statue of Eros in the center of Piccadilly Circus. The structure of timbers which had been erected around the statue in the early days of the war to protect it from bomb blasts was still in place, and people lucky enough to arrive on the scene early had climbed up to get themselves box seats for the spectacle. After about an hour Reilly and I were able to maneuver ourselves to a slightly elevated spot at the base of the statue which served as a good vantage point for us to watch the antics of the crowd.

There was a bawdy song current during World War II which almost any one alive during that era will recall—"Roll me over, Yankee soldier!" There was no set pattern to the couplets—each branch of the service had its own version, I think. I remember one eastward crossing when a returning paratrooper

sang over a hundred verses to that song without repeating anything except the chorus, which went "Roll me over, lay me
down, and do it again." That night in Piccadilly Circus hundreds of thousands of voices belted out this ditty, often singing
different verses, but all those hundreds of thousands of voices
swelling to a thundering crescendo at each repetition of the
chorus. I sang bass—Dean Reilly sang Iowa cornfield. It didn't
matter.

As we stood shoulder to shoulder observing the celebration,
the street lights muted by the wafting cloud of blue smoke
from a half million cigarettes, an object suddenly struck me
squarely in the chest. Instinctively I snatched at the thing in
mid-air as it continued to fall. My first thought was "grenade!"
But immediately I realized it was too small and soft and slick.
Reilly had caught sight of the object when it struck me.

"What the hell!" he exclaimed.

I opened my hand and I was holding—a Damson plum. I
looked up and perched high above us in the crowd of lucky ones
who had gotten box seats on the superstructure protecting the
statue was a smiling girl with a bag of plums in her hand.

"How 'bout one for my buddy?" I suggested.

"Righto!" she called back over the din, and down came another plum with the girl herself following close behind, giving
up her high-up vantage point in the process.

The farm boy in me came out then.

"These are delicious. Did you grow them?" It would be hard
to come up with any more inane remark, but that's what I said.

"No, I didn't—I have a friend with a plum tree who gave
them to me."

We introduced ourselves, and, unbelievably, in the midst of
that throng of revellers the three of us talked, or rather the
girl, whose name was Valerie, talked, pouring out the story of
her life quite matter-of-factly while Reilly and I listened.

Some Nazi public relations fellow came up with the term
"blitzkreig" ("blitz" being German for lightning and "kreig"
for war) to describe Hitler's quick and successful strikes
against neighboring countries in the early years of the war.

The English had shortened this to "blitz," which came to the western world to denote the aerial assault on the British Isles. Valerie was fifteen years old when the London blitz began. Her father was a regular in the British Army, and had been sent to Palestine before the war started. British military service was a no-frills affair in those days which didn't include provision for families to accompany men assigned to foreign duty, so Valerie and her mother and younger brother eked out an existence on his less than munificent pay in a small flat in an industrial section of London.

The blitz began, and when the air raid sirens sounded everyone who was not manning an anti-aircraft gun or searchlight, or doing fire fighting or rescue work, was expected to go underground. One evening the family was just sitting down to a scanty dinner when they heard the familiar warning notes. The mother urged Valerie and her brother to " 'urry up and get it in your tummies before Jerry does us all in," but they were too hungry to leave the food sitting on the table. When the bomb hit, Valerie's mother was killed instantly, her younger brother was blown out into the street, both legs shattered, and Valerie herself was buried alive with a broken arm and multiple minor cuts. She described the horror of two nights lying terrified and helpless under a mass of debris, with the earth shaking around her and the rubble settling and shifting over her aching body. She described the effort it took to shift her head in one direction or another to search for open spaces in the mass of material which would allow her to breathe. She described the anguish of hearing the constant drone of bombers overhead and the whistle of falling bombs, and not being able to tell how close they were . . . the despair of not hearing any rescue teams working near the spot where she was trapped. And of course the agony of not knowing what had happened to her mother and younger brother. Perhaps it wasn't the time or the place to hear this kind of story, but it was the first time Valerie had ever been able to talk about it to anyone, she said. Remembering, she would be overwhelmed by grief, and would cry for a few minutes, and then she would continue, her voice devoid of emotion. So we continued to listen. Eventually the recue teams did find her, and Valerie was reunited with her brother. An elderly neighbor, a Mrs. Frommer, who had half a house still standing, gave Valerie and her brother shelter. The young boy could get around on crutches at the time we talked to Valerie in 1945 but he still was unable to walk, and she had been told he would never walk again. For some reason which I don't recall she didn't get her father's family allotment after the bomb hit her home, and she desperately needed money for food and fuel. Someone suggested Valerie get in the "Land Army," an organization of young people who worked on the farms of England, and Valerie would have liked this, but her brother was terrified of being separated from her. Another friend, an older girl, was supporting her elderly parents by her earnings as a prostitute and she suggested that Valerie try earning a living this way.

So at the age of fifteen, Valerie entered the world's oldest profession, and in her opinion became quite successful at it. With her earnings she was able to support the three of them, herself, her crippled brother and the neighbor, Mrs. Frommer.

Because so much of my time as a medic had been given over to administering penicillin to GIs who had contracted venereal diseases from some of these "Piccadilly Commandos," as they were known to the men, I asked Valerie if she had ever had any problem of this nature. Quite matter of factly she related that she had been rounded up with a group of girls and treated at a public clinic for gonorrhea. The nurse in charge had given her a particularly rough verbal going over for not getting treated sooner, but Valerie said she had been completely unaware that she was infected.

I asked Valerie if she had ever been in love, really in love, and then I could have bitten my tongue. She began sobbing uncontrollably, and I tried to apologize. She said it was all right, his name was Ronnie. He was a tail gunner on a B-17. The entire bomber crew would get a twenty-four hour pass and hightail it for London where they would rent a suite at a good hotel, and then get in touch with Valerie and her girl friend, the older girl who had suggested prostitution to Valerie in the first place. The two girls "lived in" with the bomber crew until their twenty-four hours ran out. Valerie described the twenty-four hours as being "very busy" for her. Then when the crew's leave was up the airmen would take off for the base and Valerie and her friend would hit the streets again.

The only problem was, Valerie had fallen for Ronnie, who had shyly told her he loved her, and that when the war was over they would get married and forget the past and live happily ever after in a beautiful place called "Montana."

That was before the 1,000 plane Allied air raid on Schweinfurt, Germany, a town where ninety per cent of the ball bearings which went into Nazi planes and tanks and trucks were made.[11] The saturation bombing was successful, but a frightful price was paid. The bombers had to fly over the front lines in France and deep into Germany, with the Luftwaffe dogging them all the way in and out. Ronnie was one of those who paid the price. Valerie learned about it when a different bomb crew put in an appearance in London almost a month later. Her dream of becoming a Montana housewife perished. She asked me then if Montana was really as beautiful as Ronnie had described it, and I said yes, every bit as beautiful. I had never been to Montana, but I figured the Lord wasn't going to charge me with that one small fib in any heavenly balancing of the books.

Later I asked Valerie if she had ever been mistreated by any of her customers, or if she had ever been in any real danger hawking her wares in the blacked-out and fog-ridden streets of

---

11. Ed. note: In the October 14, 1943 raid on the ball bearing plants at Schweinfurt when the Americans did not have the advantage of long-range fighter protection, the cost in men and planes was enormous: sixty of the 291 American bombers were destroyed. This resulted in a dispute between the Allies, and, unfortunately, when the combined English-American attack was made with 1,000 planes four months later, the German ball bearing industry had already been dispersed, so the attack did not accomplish its primary purpose. See Winston S. Churchill, *Closing the Ring*, Houghton Mifflin Company, Boston, 1951 (pp.522-23).

London (I was remembering tales I had heard about Jack the
Ripper, of course).

First she told us about the many times she had been robbed.
Who were they, I asked, the men who robbed her—Americans?
Australians? Canadians?

"No, mostly our blokes," she said. "And they always lec-
tured me about what I was doing. Trying to clear their con-
sciences, I guess."

In response to the other part of my question she said there
had been only one time when she had been in danger.

"It was one of our blokes again. I picked 'im up on a back
street near Rainbow Corner, and 'e seemed like a right enough
fellow, until of a sudden 'e began screamin' something about
the wrath of the Lord and started slyshing at my left breast
with a knife. I ran. 'E ran after me, screamin' foul nymes, but I
knew the streets better than 'e did, so I managed to escape. But
then I thought I was going to bleed to death before I got to a
clinic."

"How bad a wound was it, and what did they do for it," I
asked.

She turned away from the crowd, slipped between Reilly
and me for privacy, and opened her blouse to expose surpris-
ingly beautiful little breasts about the size of Valencia oranges.
The area surrounding the nipple of the left breast, though, had
a terribly ugly scar, about twelve inches long, beginning above
the breast and continuing diagonally down on to her chest. I
stared in the half light at one of the lousiest jobs of surgical
stitching I had ever seen. Someone had editorialized his resent-
ment of her trade in his handling of the surgical needle. My anger must have been apparent, because she made haste to
explain what had happened.

"The surgeon wasn't very kind, y'know. 'E said if 'e 'ad a
daughter like me, 'e'd run 'er clear out of London."

"I'll tell you what our Major Freund would have done to
anyone who had done such a lousy job. He'd have taken the
hide off his body," I said, "and then he'd have scrubbed and
done the job right."

I told Valerie the terribly uneven scar could be revised without too much involvement if she chose to secure help, but she shook her head in resignation. Obviously, she'd had a belly full of the medical profession.

As Valerie was fastening her blouse, and I was pondering what we could do to help her, Reilly gave me a little shake on the shoulder to get my attention.

"Cope, listen to what the guy is sayin' over the horn."

Bad news. The victory announcement was premature. We had been celebrating in response to a false report. A million people began melting away in almost total silence. We told Valerie goodbye and joined the mob bearing in the direction of Victoria Station. A very long time later we were able to get on board a crowded train for Southampton. We were both so engrossed in our own thoughts that not a word passed between us on the return trip. Finally, as we walked out of the station and down High Street I stopped and turned to my friend.

"Reilly," I said, "this has been a helluva night. Suppose, just suppose, that when Valerie struck up an acquaintance with us tonight the ripe plum had been a grenade and the three of us had been killed in the explosion. Now we're up at those pearly gates where St. Peter decides who comes in and who stays out. What do you think would have taken place?"

Without a moment's hesitation Reilly said, "Cope, I'll tell you what I think—I think he'd say for us gents to step aside and let the little lady come on in first."

I nodded in total agreement, and we lapsed into silence again as we walked over the cobblestones towards the Gray Ghost riding quietly dockside. Even the customs men at the gangplank were glum that night.

V-J Day, finally

John Bobb and I were the only ones who showed up for breakfast the next morning. A gloom seemed to pervade the

whole ship. Even Old Bob, our British waiter, was not his usual
cheery self.

After breakfast John and I went back to A143. Red Stewart,
from Lubbock, Texas, a clerk on our staff, was playing a song
called "Marie" on his record player, over and over again. Rube
Wrablik, our resident artist, was finishing a crayon portrait.
Ed Nash, another clerk, was playing solitaire. Reilly was lying
on his top bunk staring at the ceiling. Maybe he was thinking
about Valerie, too. Certainly she was on my mind all that day.

In the early evening Bill Roush and Pontzious left the ship
to walk down High Street to the Red Cross canteen. About
8:00 o'clock the ship's public address system came on with a
BBC announcement to standby for an address by the prime
minister.

And shortly thereafter the PM came on the air and announced the unconditional surrender of the Japanese and the
end of World War II.

And then pandemonium did break out. Someone had
stashed away a fifth of bourbon for just such an occasion, and
it was brought out and passed around. Towards 11:00 p.m. I
took a turn on the Boat Deck and saw what looked like an air
battle over Southampton. Anti-aircraft searchlights swept the
sky relentlessly. I heard the series of staccato reports which
were the telltale sound of anti-aircraft gunfire, and saw shells
exploding thousands of feet up over the city. I was situated in
front of the bridge where two junior officers were standing regular port watch. One of them, carried away by the excitement
of the occasion, went out to the docking bridge and fired a Very
pistol several times. These pistols were designed to send flares
several hundred feet skyward and were useful in disasters at
sea to attract rescuers. This night the officer didn't pay attention to the direction of his aim. The flare hit a small wooden
structure in the dock area which caught fire, and it took some
time for the fire brigade to extinguish the flames. I watched
this for awhile and then went back to A143 to see what was going on with my buddies there.

Jack Sigmond, our man who had thrown the cups in the hospital galley some months before, had gone bonkers again. This time he seized upon anything that looked like Army issue, and was chucking it out through the porthole into the Solent River, and before anyone realized what was going on, he had collected and disposed of thousands of dollars worth of clothing and equipment for which we were all individually responsible.

Somehow we got him calmed down. But Reilly never did get out of his bunk that day or evening. And the next morning we began loading troops for the trip home.

And the last time

In January of 1946 the hospital staff of the *Queen Mary* had shrunk to a complement of six men—and we were all non-smokers. But by the time the ship drydocked in Southampton in early January of 1946, we non-smokers had, through the courtesy of gift cartons from the Red Cross and the cheap prices at the PX, managed to squirrel away seventy cartons of cigarettes which, we were told, at the going rate of exchange in Europe, was worth almost $1,000.00 in cash on the market. We were literally licking our lips in anticipation of our second trip to Paris and all the fun we could have with so much wampum at our disposal.

But then disaster struck. Our officers preceded us by a few hours at 14th Port Headquarters, and were handed an Armed Forces directive permitting passage from the UK to the Continent for only two persons from any unit in any given month! We were dumbstruck—and to make matters worse, no one seemed to know what had prompted the restriction. Even Sgt. Moon Mullins, who *always* knew the inmost secrets of the workings of the military machine, was at a loss. All he could say was, "Fellers, the henhouse door is closed!"

Our officers headed for London; the rest of us stayed on the *Queen*, which, in drydock, without any heat in the coldest month of the year, wasn't exactly like living in the bridal suite at the Ritz.

That same night Master Sergeant Fogarty, from the London Motor Pool, showed up at our quarters. He had come to pick up the baby stuff we always got for him when we were in New York. We asked him about the new travel restrictions and Fogarty said the lid was really on, but no one seemed to know why. He said our officers had really gotten the London brass hot under the collar when they tried some political strong-arming.

"Just lay low," he advised us, "until the officers give up. Go to Bournemouth for a couple of days and then come back to the ship and wait for me. I'll get back with you as soon as I can do some dealing. Don't give up on me."

So we followed his advice and took a two-day excursion down the coast to Bournemouth, a peace-time resort city. Here we saw evidence of some of the preparations the British had made in anticipation of a German invasion. Tank traps were spaced along the sandy beaches three or four miles each way from the Bournemouth quay, close enough to stop vehicles, or to delay them long enough for gunfire to sight in on them. Messages in chalk and paint offered various suggestions for Hitler's personal demise, and other graffiti were less than welcoming to the invading armies.

In a little snug harbor I found a restroom, or W.C., as the British term these convenient way stations, which suited my peculiar needs of the moment. The customary English toilet at that time was an antique by American standards. The water reservoir (the English called it a "blighty"), instead of being just behind the toilet, was hung high on the wall, with a pull chain hanging down to trip a valve which activated the flushing mechanism. On the facing wall in this W.C. was the most elegant bit of graffiti I have ever run across in my many years of travelling and using facilities in all different climes and conditions: the inscription etched in most elegant Old English style letters, by a real artist with the point of a bayonet, read:

Yea, Verily, Doth
The Swinging Chain
Denote A Warm Seat

When the six of us got back from Bournemouth the next day
we found a note taped to the door of A143 signed by our friend,
Master Sergeant Fogarty, telling us to be patient a bit longer,
and for two more days we shivered and shook as the *Queen* was
being pummeled and scraped and painted while perched on gigantic stilts in the dry dock basin. In the early evening of the
second day Al Draper and I were walking to the Red Cross
Canteen on High Street to get a sandwich, when the driver of a
Jeep headed in our direction began sounding his horn repeat-
edly. It was Fogarty, and we piled into the Jeep with him and
rode back to A143 to hear what he said was good news.

When we had rejoined our friends Fogarty pulled six sets of
military orders from his brief case, and the six of us became instant members of a military medical detachment of the 14th
Port. We were ordered to proceed immediately by aircraft to
Paris to effect the relief of the medical detachment numbered
so-and-so at Villacoublay Airfield outside Paris. The orders really looked good, and we were concerned that we might get
stuck in Paris working as medics until the real medical unit
showed up. Fogarty set us straight. The orders were totally
phony, he said. But we would be all right so long as we didn't
get close to any military installations, not even a mess hall, and
kept our noses clean and didn't get picked up by the Paris
gendarmarie.

So off we headed for London in the early morning fog. We
had packed all seventy cartons of cigarettes in my duffel bag (I
was the lucky one, due to a selection made by picking straws
made of tongue depressors—call me "Shortstraw Bob") and believe me, we had to stuff hard to get them all in one duffel bag.
We knew enough about smuggling cigarettes to know that it
would be a dead giveaway to have square edges showing on the
rounded outside of the bag, so we used blankets for padding. I
refused to use my blankets for this purpose—bad enough to do

time at Wormwood Scrubs without also having a charge of absconding with Army property hanging over me—so we used Louis Macaronas' blankets; but I didn't feel a whole lot better about it when he began carefully removing his identification from them.

The fog prevailed, and all aircraft were grounded for that day. Waiting patiently at Bovingdon Airdrome, we slept fitfully, always aware of the contraband bag, and each of us taking turns at keeping one arm through the carrying straps. I kept dreaming about how good the blanket in that bag would feel wrapped around my shivering body, but none of us was willing to take that kind of risk.

Next morning the weather had worsened and we were cursing our bad luck. A crisp and courteous voice over the PA kept adding to the long list of cities which were fogged-in: Antwerp, Berlin, Frankfort, Lisbon, Paris, all indefinitely closed. Another crisp and courteous voice kept paging a particular unit: "Will the relief medical unit of 14th Port bound for Villacoublay please report to operations at once!" We must have heard that call five or six times, and just as a light flashed in my brain Bill Roush grabbed me and yelled, "Hey, that's us!"

It was Fogarty on the line. He said he had new orders so we could go by what the English call "boat train." We were relieved. The days had slipped away, and if we were to get to Paris again it would have to be now or never. The *Queen* was due out of drydock that very day and scheduled to sail on the third morning, and here we were, still in London.

The train part of the boat train moved at a snail's pace through the heavy fog, to Newhaven, England where we boarded the *Isle of Chenelsworth* (maybe 300 × 20 feet) for the channel crossing.

I was not skilled at the game of international smuggling, but I was determined to learn, and I had some able teachers. For starters, we had a massive padlock on the hasp of the duffel bag, but Shortstraw Bob didn't carry the key. No sir, no way. Al Shriner was the possessor of the key, which he had carefully secreted in the toe of his left shoe (which, naturally, caused

him to walk with a limp); and he and my other co-conspirators
were going through customs inspection in a line as far as possible removed from the line I was standing in.

I thought the customs inspector I had picked looked to be a
pretty good egg, but I was wrong. Good eggs and customs men
are mutually exclusive concepts. The one I had picked was actually meaner than a striped snake when stepped on.

"All right, Yank, let's 'ave a look."

"There it is, sir. Medical supplies for our relief mission to
Villacoublay. Running late we are, on account of the fog. I
hope we get there in time to help."

Cool as a hog on ice, I was.

It didn't wash. My Good Egg was flapping away at the padlock, getting angrier by the second. I pointed to the chalk-
marked phony identification, and looking towards the ship
saw five anxious faces watching every movement. They had
less reason for feeling nervous than I did. I was on the verge of
wetting my trousers.

Attack seemed my only recourse. I harangued the poor man
unmercifully while he continued to struggle with the padlock. I
talked about how shabbily the English treated men who
should be headed state-side on the way to being de-mobbed
(their word); how, having performed beyond the call of duty,
we were now sent backtracking by an ungrateful ally to treat
victims of an epidemic at Villacoublay, France, at great risk to
our own health; how we had been harassed and nit-picked by
an official of that government we had been assisting (I didn't
say who), which government and country we had, until now,
considered our friends and allies, even to the death, etc., etc.,
ad nauseum.

"And so, sir, if you will continue to hold this bag of most essential life-saving devices and supplies at your own risk, of
course, and if you will guard it with your life, I will go on board
the ship to search for our officer, and I shall at once return
with him and the key to this container, and we shall remove,
once and for all, any and all suspicion from your mind, but I
still recognize that you are only doing your duty and commend

you for your vigilance, and am grateful that this war has ended and yet left men of your caliber guarding frontiers with the selfless devotion to duty that you exhibit."

And so saying, I took a deep breath and started away in the general direction of the gangplank.

"I say, no, my good chap, 'old up a bit. Now what we 'ave 'ere is all official items."

"Yes, sir, it's mainly the newly-developed antitoxin called questaframastan "A", along with the frenellin preservative and the Dnalepoc applicator," I answered helpfully.

"Oh, well, it's all official stuff then, 'ere ya go, Yank, and 'ave a syfe journey."

And so saying he chalked his magic initials on the duffel bag, and I no longer felt a consuming need to go to the bathroom. And for the record, neither the antitoxin nor the preservative existed, then or now, except in the imagination of one medic with his back-to-the-wall, and the Dnalepoc applicator comes from spelling "Copeland" backwards and tacking it on to an non-existent, but extremely useful, medical device.

I marched triumphantly up the gangplank and was immediately surrounded by five jubilant companions. And within minutes thereafter I learned the "rest of the story'—I had been set up in the straw-drawing contest. All the other fellows had two straws, one long and one short. Once again I had been flim-flammed. But I did gain some stature from the experience. After that my buddies were convinced I had a golden tongue and could talk my way out of anything.

We stashed the duffel bag and began looking around the Isle of Whatchamacallit and found our first impression correct: she was like a Virginia cheroot cigar, long and very slim. She also had metal buckets hanging on wooden pegs just about everywhere. Being an expert on channel crossings by virtue of my one prior experience, I said the buckets were probably filled with sand to fight fires from bombs during the war. The one among us with the rich accent that smacked of cornpone and barbecue, and who also happened to be tall, stood on tiptoe, looked into the buckets, and gave the lie to my explanation.

"Hunh-unh, Cope, they're empty." Al Draper said.

But they did not remain empty for long. The fog became lighter as we headed for Dieppe. The wind started blowing harder, and the seas got choppier. One of the seaman, in a perfect example of the understatement for which the English are noted, allowed as how we were in for a squall. The Virginia cheroot was half in and half out of the water; the propellor would whack at the air when the stern came up out of the deep, and what the whack of the propellor did to passengers was much like what a terrier does to a dead rat—it shook the veritable stuffin's out of us. For the second time, I got seasick, but when I reached for a bucket it was too late, they were all taken and were being used. It was truly touching, though, to see Macaronas and Bill Roush sharing the same metal container. I don't think they were ever spiritually closer than they were at that moment. And it was on this very crossing that history records one of the most poignant messages ever communicated by a soldier to his first sergeant when Macaronas, Louis T., said to Roush, William, "Bill, I've got the dry heaves."

Eventually all tribulations come to an end, and this one did too. We were informed that the trip had taken three times as long as it normally did, and I fervently believed that, but the sad part was that now our time in Paris was even further eroded.

There was no searching by French officials at the Dieppe end of the trip. I believe we could have driven an armored tank off the ship without being questioned, which was fortunate because I don't think if we had been challenged, any one of the six of us non-smokers could have mustered up enough French to ask for a light.

When Nicky Brodsky, our London song composer friend, learned that we were going back to Paris he promised us an introduction to his boyhood chum, Michel Gharmatny, director of the Folies Bergére. Nicky had assured us that Gharmatny would be delighted to give us top dollar for all our cartons of cigarettes, so acting on the prospects of tomorrow's financial well-being, we felt totally relaxed about checking into two rooms at the Hôtel de Chateaudun, and the biggest thrill of the evening for the three guys in Room #24 was calling Zuzu at the switchboard and asking for "nombre vingt cinq." So much for the big time operators from the *Queen Mary*!

The next morning, feeling that I had done my share by carrying my weight through English customs, I made the other five blokes share the burden of lugging the duffel bag to the Folies Bergére, and Al Draper had the honor of bearing the large envelope with Brodsky's letter of introduction to M. Gharmatny. M. Gharmatny was as good to us as Brodsky had promised he would be. First he shelled out about half a bushel of franc notes, equivalent to about $980, which we split six ways, and then he gave us complimentary box seats to the matinée performance.

And let me tell you, that was some show. We all kind of felt sorry for the female entertainers, though. They were so lovely, those girls, and they smiled a lot, and they looked to be well-fed, because they were all curves everywhere, but the poor brave things were forced to work almost naked because of the clothing shortage. Not true, I noticed, of the few men in the show: they seemed to have garments of a sufficient weight to cover them and keep out the cold. And when M. Gharmatny took us backstage at intermission and introduced us to some of the entertainers, we six army medics were so preoccupied and distressed by the girls' pitiable, destitute, unclothed condition we had trouble recalling our own names, ranks and serial numbers. But then, one must remember, we were operating under forged orders, and that might account for such temporary lapses . . .

We split up after the matinée. Sergeant Macaronas and I had been talking about Villacoublay Airfield and the "terrible epidemic" I had described to the British customs guard. We didn't realize until we looked at a map that the field was actually on the outskirts of Paris, and we both had an unaccounted-for desire to go there, perhaps an unconscious wish to give our trip some façade of legitimacy. In any event, whatever the reason, with our pockets loaded with more than $150 in franc notes we elected to spend some of those francs on a bus that would take us to the airfield.

When the bus started off the engine sounded kind of funny and I found out why the first time we hit an upgrade. Everybody had to get out and push. The bus was propelled by a charcoal burner of some kind attached to the rear. I drifted back to get a good look at the power plant just as we topped the grade, and my clinical curiosity almost got me left behind. But since I operated much like a bus myself and always did a bit better going downhill I caught up in time. And I was a wiser man when we got out to push the bus up the next hill; the pushing took enough out of us, I didn't want to have to do any more running to catch up.

When we got off the bus at the entrance to Villacoublay Mac said, "Man, what a hell of an epidemic."

There had, indeed, been an epidemic here, but Fogarty had sent us too late. Piles of torn and partly-burned aircraft lay in windrows on two sides of the main field, rusted chunks of British Hurricanes and Lancasters, skeletons of American P-38s, Thunderbolts and Flying Fortresses, and some wrecked German planes, too. We stood in silence for a few moments, surveying this monumental tribute to the megalomania of one man, and I think Mac and I were probably sharing some of the same thoughts, remembering that in each of those planes there had been young men, courageous young men doing a job, patrolling skies far distant from their own homes, full of hopes about the future and a determination to get the war over and done with, young men with families and friends who would miss them terribly. It was a sobering moment in time for each of us.

But youth and life cannot be denied, and all that pushing the bus up hills had taken its toll of our energies. By the time we got to Villacoublay Mac and I were not just hungry, we were starved—or so we described it to each other. Fogarty had warned us not to go to any military establishments, but when we came upon a sizeable building with a sign indicating it was a

U.S. Armed Forces mess hall, our empty stomachs conquered discretion.

And just as Fogarty had forewarned, with our salivary glands responding to all sorts of delightful aromas concocted by the French chefs hired by the Americans, we were met, just inside the door and at the very gates of heaven, by a tall and formidable appearing MP.

"See your orders, please," he demanded, holding out his hand.

We pulled out those lovely, albeit phony, orders, and as he perused them I began expounding on the success of our mission and the life-saving medications we had only recently delivered, the new antibiotic, questaframastan "A", and its miracle properties.

"Our people know about this?" he asked.

"My goodness, yes, they've been most helpful," I replied, and Mac, the honest Greek, nodded vigorously.

"OK, guys, eat up," he said, waving us on to the chow line. "We have to check real close, you know. There's one hell of a lot of free loaders trying to get in here to eat since the war is over."

And we thanked him and headed for the food. What a boon, I thought, to have developed these wonderful new medicines like questaframastan "A", and new devices like the Dnalepoc applicator which provided us a courtesy pass to the most exclusive places.

But our joy was short-lived, and not for the reasons Fogarty had given. The main dining room had windows fronting on the sidewalk, and there were no blinds on them. The dining room was crowded, but the choicest seats near the windows were nearly all vacant, so we took our well-filled trays there and sat down to enjoy the abundance. I bent down over my plate and dug in with gusto, but after the first few bites, I leaned back in my chair to eat more slowly and enjoy the various subtle flavors. It was then I glanced casually out the window and saw dozens of emaciated Frenchmen on the sidewalk outside the building, watching us hungrily. Each of them seemed to be

looking directly at me. After that Mac and I continued eating
with our eyes downcast and fixed on our plates, and only desultory conversation passed between us. For some reason each
mouthful of food took an effort to swallow. We couldn't move
to another location in the dining room, that would have been
too obvious; we couldn't leave anything on our plates—that
would have been an insult to their hunger. So, in intermittent
silence, we labored on over those plates, which suddenly
seemed burdened with a great deal more than we wanted to
eat, and when we had finished left the mess hall and headed
back for the bus stop as quickly as possible.

Mac and I were the first to return to the Hôtel de
Chateaudun, and while we sat in our room talking about starving people and dead people and wasted resources and man's in-
humanity to man, the other fellows showed up, all excited over
what they had seen at the Louvre, Notre-Dame, L'étoile and
some of the other cultural attractions of Paris. They thought
Mac and I had been nuts to go to Villacoublay, and I guess
they were right.

All those francs were burning holes in our pockets, and we
were told that the Place Vendôme was the place to spend
them. Dozens of names I had only been remotely aware of
hung on placards over the shops on this beautiful, paved plaza:
Chanel, Lanvin, Coty. We got off the bus and lingered at the
bus stop trying to decide where to go first when a sleek, chauf-
feur-driven Rolls Royce pulled up in front of the Lanvin building. We did a triple double-take when two perfectly-groomed
French poodles were first assisted out of the car by the chauffeur, who controlled them by leashes held in his left hand, at
the same time extending his right hand to assist first the Duke,
and then the Duchess, of Windsor from the limousine.

Now we knew where we wanted to do our shopping! As soon
thereafter as common courtesy allowed we went inside Lanvin
and asked one of the clerks what fragrance the Duchess of
Windsor preferred. Then each of us purchased an ounce of the
same very, very expensive *parfum*, in the case of Bill Roush
and myself, as presents for our wives, and for the other four,

who knows? fish bait or ransom, or would the precious bottles go to mothers and sisters?

And then we had to head back for Dieppe, and from there back to England, Southampton and our *Queen*. But this time, before we left Dieppe, Bill Roush, our schoolteacher from California, led us on a history class field trip of the waterfront, reminding us that Dieppe was the place where hundreds of commandos, some British, some American, but the great majority of them Canadian, had died in a preliminary attack to test whether a full-scale invasion of Hitler's Fortress Europe would be feasible.

And so ended our second visit to Paris.

Chapter 8
PRISONERS OF WAR

The five thousand

In October of 1945 there were only three of us medics left to work our ward on the *Queen*, John Bobb, Al Fortmuller and myself.

I had a three-day 500-mile pass, and as I had done before, I stretched it into a three-day 1,450-mile pass. Since I almost always travelled home via the thumb, I was usually pretty exhausted by the time I got back to the ship. This particular time was worse than usual. I had hitched a ride with a trucker who was dead tired and asked me to take over the wheel for him, so instead of being able to catch up on my sleep, I drove the truck all the way from the Pennsy Turnpike to the Lincoln Tunnel while he slept.

I left my truck driver friend at the tunnel exit and hoofed it down to the waterfront. When I was about two blocks away from Pier 90 I was startled to see a large number of strange-looking men coming out of the "ptomaine junctions" along 12th Avenue, carrying handfuls of food. Strange-looking, because they were all emaciated and hollow-cheeked, with sunken eyes and protruding bones. They wore various combinations of borrowed Army attire. Some of them limped; many of them were drunk. Then I saw Army trucks coming in off

12th Avenue bringing more of these bedraggled creatures. A few had articles wrapped in canvas, some had what appeared to be Japanese flags wrapped around slender pieces of tubing. And other men were just plodding along, carrying nothing at all. They all seemed to be headed towards Pier 90.

Still totally bewildered, I went straight to the hospital. John Bobb was already there. He had returned a half hour earlier, and was trying to calm a small group of these living cadavers who had apparently been directed by ship's personnel to report to the hospital as soon as they boarded.

John looked to be in a state of shock. He brightened when I entered and said, "Bob, I'm sure glad to see you. These fellows say they are what is left of the men captured at Singapore in '42. I've never seen anything like it. Looks like we're going to have our hands full this trip."

I remembered when Singapore had fallen. It had been such a shock to the free world. We *knew* Singapore was impregnable. It was protected by the British Navy and the British Navy was invincible. Except three days after Pearl Harbor the Japanese sank *H.M.S. Prince of Wales* and *H.M.S. Repulse* off the Malayan coast and gained control of the seas east of Malaya. In early January, 1942 the Japs began daylight air raids on Singapore and quickly gained air superiority. On February 8th they started landing troops on the west side of the island and took over Tengah airfield, and about the same time landed another force west of the causeway connecting the island to the mainland.

On February 15, 1942 the British commandant, General Percival, finally surrendered the 130,000 local, British, Australian and Indian troops who were defending the island. These men, and most of the foreign nationals and refugees resident in Singapore who had either not heeded the warning signs and left with evacuation ships, or who were required to stay for some reason, were rounded up by the Japanese and sent to concentration camps, to endure four years of starvation, disease, hard labor and heinous mistreatment, unless death shortened their term of captivity. Death had indeed shortened captivity for the majority. What we had on board were 5,000 European troops who had somehow survived.

"Are you men all British?" I asked.

"Mostly," said one fellow with a left leg six inches shorter than its mate, "but there are a mixin' of French and Dutch and a Belgian or two, I think."

"Do you have an M.O., a medical officer in charge?" I asked.

"Lordy, I don't know. We've been 'ere and there, first on ship, then to your west coast, then into 'ospitals and onto trains to a camp in New Jersey, and some of us into 'ospital again. And now wiv lorries, we got 'ere," my informant explained.

More and more came in. John and I tried to sort out the ones who seemed in the worst condition. I hailed a ship's engineer officer who customarily cut through the hospital going to and from the engine room. I pointed at the group of shattered men, milling about the antechamber.

"Most of these are your chaps who were overrun by the Japs at Singapore in '42," I said. "We're covered up here, we've just the three of us. Would you mind going to the PA room and have them put out an urgent call for doctors, medics, any officer, just anyone who could help us ..."

"Lord God Almighty! I cawn't believe me eyes. Roight away ..." And he hurried off, looking backward once, his eyes full of pity as he headed for the stairway.

Minutes later the public address system began a series of peremptory calls. "Officer in charge of the boarding contingent report to medic in Troop Hospital. Urgent, repeat, urgent."

Time passed, and no one came, but we did what we could. Some of the men who were able helped by spreading the linen on the beds assigned to them. Others, and there were many of them, had lost touch with reality altogether. These men just faced the walls, or lay on the deck, oblivious to our frenetic activity. A few of them had too much liquor from the brief, happy lark on 12th Avenue, their first taste of freedom in four years.

Had we been fully staffed, as we were before the war ended, every man who limped or shuffled through our swinging door would have been admitted. They were all candidates for medical assistance and treatment. But that night John Bobb and Bob Copeland had to turn scores away and take only the most serious cases. Those we turned away didn't complain. They hadn't been pampered.

Midnight came, and Albert Fortmuller reported in. Albert lived in the Bronx and had been recently assigned to the Medical Corps from another branch of the Army. But whatever Al lacked in technical knowledge and ability, he more than made up for in compassion. And that's the first requirement for a good medic.

Towards morning some of the mentally deranged men began creating problems. They thought John and Al and I were either Japs or Koreans and, frightened, they would respond to a gentle hand on the shoulder by going into hysterics. Some would fall to the deck trying to get away from us. One poor soul even tore three fingernails loose clawing at the steel deck of the ship where the wooden wall divided two of our wards. I carried him to the operating room easily. He only weighed about ninety pounds, and this was after he had been getting U.S. Army chow, on ships, trains, and at hospitals, for weeks.

It's a good thing we had a lot of morphine Syrettes and other supplies. We had to do our own diagnosing and prescribing, John Bobb and I. We gave penicillin to those infected in one way or the other, put sulfa on any open wound, gave morphine to the mentally disturbed, and ADP pills to those who were sick from the booze, or the booze combined with the roll of the ship.

About daylight three stragglers came in. The middle man of the trio was being assisted by the others. To look at the blood and gore covering his face, head and shoulders you would have thought he had survived a mangled beheading. Not so. What had happened was this: these three men, left to their own devices for several hours before they were due on shipboard had ranged far into the heart of Manhattan, drinking a lot but eating even more. Finally they were rounded up by the police, who escorted them personally to the ship. They had started up the gangplank when the one who was so badly injured had lost his balance and plunged head first twelve or fifteen feet downward onto the heavy, oak-timbered float which kept the *Queen* from getting too close to the pier.

I wished the Pier Guards had sent him to Halloran General. Instead they directed him to us. I hadn't even cleaned up the mess from the ripped fingernail job yet. John and Al were both busy with other patients so they couldn't help; well, I would clean him up to see how bad it was, and if surgery was definitely indicated, I would send him over to Halloran.

I used sponges very gently to wash off some of the blood, and it was even worse than I expected. An arc of skin was ripped open from the left hair line across to the top of the zygomatic process, the little flat edge along the side of the eye. The gash cut all the way down to the skull. It was clearly a job for Halloran, but when I told the patient I was going to have to send him there he began sobbing and pleading to stay on the *Queen Mary*. He seemed terrified of being separated from his two buddies.

I looked at the cut again, and wondered whether it was fair to him to do the job myself. And then suddenly I felt my body adjusting to the movement of the ship, and the question became moot. We were under way. I had been so intent on what I was doing that I had not heard the final calls over the PA.

I put a moist pressure bandage on the man's skull, and left the three of them in the OR and rang up the PA room. I got my friend, Albert, a British ship's officer (also the *Queen's* official photographer) on the line, and he told me he was sure there was a doctor assigned from the British Army Medical Corps on board. I heaved a sigh of relief, and asked him to send out an urgent request for the British M.O. again, this time emphasizing there was an emergency surgery imminent.

Just then one of the mates of the injured man ran out of the OR screaming, "'e's chokin' to death, doc!"

He was right. The injured man was lying face upwards on the deck between the sink and the operating table, his eyes wide open and bulging like ping pong balls. His feast from the happy tour of Manhattan was on the floor, or at least a part of it was. Although his teeth were set firmly together it was obvious he was strangling on some of the regurgitated food. I knew I would need help, so I did the only thing I could think of: I asked the two friends who had brought the man in to stay and assist me.

The two men helped flop the strangling man up on the operating table face downward. I found then that I was unable to open his jaws. He was in a state of analgesic spasm.

If I couldn't think of something, the box score of passengers was going to change real quick. I told my two helpers they would have to stand on the operating table, but I had to give each a boost to get them up there—they weren't in the best physical condition themselves. Then, with one man at each end of the table, standing unsteadily because of the light roll of the ship, the three of us maneuvered the now cyanotic patient into a head down, feet up in the air position. I tried with every ounce of strength I had to open the clenched jaws. No luck.

Suddenly I thought of the instrument cabinet. Something had to be there. I looked, and there was that vaginal retractor that had caused me so much amusement on my first crossing on the *Queen* with 15,000 troops, none of them women. It was exactly the tool I required. My patient was missing two upper front teeth. This allowed just enough space for me to get the lip of the retractor to hold until I could twist the knob that slowly but surely forced the mouth open.

It took long forceps and then tongue depressors to clear all the peas and carrots from the man's throat. I had my assistants jostle him up and down, and then had to help them off the operating table as we laid the patient face down again.

Grabbing the oxygen mask which was always kept connected to the cylinder fastened to the bulkhead, I started forcing oxygen in, then pushing down and releasing his chest, then forcing oxygen in again, then pushing and releasing . . . on and on and on, for what seemed like an eternity, but probably wasn't more than a few minutes. The first good sign was when his head started bleeding through the compress bandage. And then, finally, what I could only regard as a miracle, an Act of God. The cyanotic tinge turned to pink, and I heard a moan.

Twenty minutes later my patient was taking deep breaths and talking to us. But the return to life also meant that the wound was bleeding again, and it was imperative that this be attended to before he suffered a severe loss of blood. Someone had to operate on the man, and there was no qualified person available. I had heard the PA periodically broadcasting an urgent call for the British Medical Officer. I got Albert in the PA room on the phone again and asked him if he had had any response. He said, no, no one had called in. I told him in my opinion we had sailed without either the British doctor or a Transport Surgeon, and that we were in for a bad time. But I also told Albert if he did, ultimately, get in touch with an M.D. to prepare him for a shock before he sent him down, because when he came to the Troop Hospital he was going to see an unqualified buck sergeant doing surgery . . . and I hung up.

I wasn't quite as confident as I sounded. It took me twice as long to prep the wound as it ordinarily would have. I didn't have any doubt that I *could* do the tying of the blood vessels and the suturing. I just knew I wasn't technically *qualified* to do it. I suppose there was some fear that a real doctor would show up at the last minute, and object to a medic's taking over a doctor's responsibility. I did explain my status (or lack of it) to the patient and his friends, and told them we had been unable to find a licensed doctor. To alleviate any anxiety I explained that, although I wasn't qualified, I had done suturing before and had no doubt about my ability or skill. I also told the patient about my concern that he might have a concussion, but said I couldn't detect any difference in the size of the pupils of his eyes or any other signs that might indicate the presence of concussion. So I felt the risk was minimal.

Then, after telling John Bobb what I was up to, I got on with the job, deadened the area and sutured the wound. I thought I did quite well—no ugly tucks or left over skin flaps. And then I bandaged the wound and carried my patient out into the ward to transfer him to a bed for the rest of the night.

But John Bobb had by that time filled all the beds. So we took the patient back to the operating room where we left him with his two companions to keep watch and John and I went searching for the unlucky fellow who we felt was least in need of attention and whose bed we could preempt. But when we looked around the ward we couldn't find it in our hearts to oust anyone. We had already screened them pretty thoroughly, and selected the men most in need of care, so there simply wasn't a man there who didn't need to be there. We solved the problem finally by scrounging up some unused mattresses, and put my surgery patient on the deck between two regular rows of beds, on several mattresses. He travelled all the way to England that way, without ever having anyone step on him, and I do believe he had the softest bed in the ward.

Then I began cleaning up the operating room. There were dirty shoe tracks and blood on the operating table cover, together with partially digested peas and carrots. There were more peas and carrots marinated in rot gut liquor on the deck. Thrown about indiscriminately were assorted sponges, suture ends, bandage rolls, hypo syringes, Kelly hemostats, scissors, and a Japanese coin. And there, in the sink, was the vaginal retractor. The very first thing I did was to pick up the vaginal retractor with the reverence it deserved, and taking the utmost care, cleaned it, sterilized it and put it gently away in the cabinet.

I had to work fast on the housekeeping, because the lack of sleep was catching up with me. I had now been running my engine full tilt for four and one-half days, with only a few short naps. And I suddenly didn't have anything left to run on. So we woke Al Fortmuller, and he worked with John while I slept, and then we let John sack out and Al and I fed the hospital patients their supper.

It took a good bit of time for the two of us to feed 200 patients, some of whom required help, but all of whom had been starved for so long, and had dreamed for so many years of nothing but food that they never wanted to stop eating. Supper lasted as long as we could get anything edible from the galley, and I must say this about the galley personnel, they really cooperated. And when the cooked food ran out, we scrounged hot tea and "biscuits" until all the tea was gone from the giant cauldron on D-Deck, and then we finally had to announce that supper was over.

Needless to say, the three of us never left the hospital area all the way to England. At least two of us needed to be awake at all times. Some of the mentally disturbed fellows still thought we were prison guards, and in one instance, while Fortmuller was napping, John Bobb saved me from a terrible blow which might have been fatal.

I had discovered a poorly-battened hatch on the port side in a short corridor between the office and the next room. I was whirling the wheel to secure the hatch, with my back to the corridor, when I heard a splintering crash and heard John yell, "Look out, Bob, he's after you!"

I barely had time to turn around. I saw this poor demented creature coming at me. He had ripped a steel bar off a bed and was swinging it over his head with the intention of bringing it down, with all the strength he had, on mine. I dived down at his feet. The steel bar hit behind my shoes as my head connected with his legs and he plunged head first into the hatch I had just secured. He was knocked unconscious, but I was, thanks to John, unhurt. We had to call in the ship's carpenter to get the bed repaired and refastened to the deck. We had gotten rather used to the appearance of our patients by this time, but the ship's carpenter was horrified by what he saw in our hospital. He just kept saying, "Oh, my Gawd! ... Oh, my Gawd!"

Paddy

Towards the end of the voyage we began to get acquainted with some of the men whose mental faculties were still intact. I was particularly interested in Paddy Parks, a native of Ireland. He nicknamed me "Bosty." I never did find out how he came up with that particular moniker. Paddy must have been a giant of a man before the war. He had been six feet eight inches tall and weighed about 14 stone— I believe that translates to around 280 pounds. When he came to us, though, he only weighed 140 pounds, stood no taller than six feet, and was bent over like an old man. Paddy told me he had been put to work in the coal mines on Formosa with a pick and a shovel and a daily quota which he described in an Irish brogue as thick as molasses: "Bosty, if oi'd a had a bloody steam lift oi couldn't have moved it all in a day!"

Paddy had the same diminutive Korean guard 365 days a year for the entire four years of his captivity. He said the formula this sadistic little man used, to arrive at the number of blows Paddy would receive at the end of each day for not filling his quota, was six whacks of the square club for each two feet of unmined coal. Paddy said he averaged twenty whacks a day.

On the human anatomy there is found in an appropriate place two mounds of muscle and fatty tissue, referred to in the plural as "buttocks." The buttocks serve a definite purpose. In fact, they have several functions, but perhaps the most important is to make the upright animal, man, comfortable when he is seated. I suppose because I was a big fellow myself, I observed that usually, the bigger the guy, the bigger the buttocks. And Paddy Parks had been no small fellow.

But in 1946 when I gave Paddy a physical while he was traveling home on the *Queen*, I found he had no buttocks at all, they had literally been beaten off of him. Only thin stringy cords showed under his mutilated skin, with small blobs of tissue at the ends, perhaps twenty of these, and that was all Paddy would have to sit on for the rest of his life.

I had an inner visceral reaction when I saw Paddy's naked backside that was like a sharp pain in the gut. We saw a great deal of suffering in the hospital, but this man's debility had been caused not by random firepower intended for an anonymous enemy, but by deliberate one-on-one brutality. There was something especially horrifying in this.

I asked Paddy if he minded if John looked, and he acquiesced. John came and looked. And John turned away, tears streaming down his face.

Paddy talked to us about the last days of the war in Asia, and the role the Americans had played.

Apparently American military commanders were very much concerned that there would be last minute mass executions of prisoners of war by the Japanese unless dramatic measures were taken to prevent this from happening. Accordingly, military strategists had pinpointed every known prisoner-of-war camp in Japan, Formosa, the Philippines, Malaya and God knows where else. Then, in one of the best-timed, most unique operations of World War II, instead of sending ground troops to the camps, they had the 11th Airborne hit all the camps at the same time, or as nearly so as possible, an operation which has been credited with saving the lives of thousands of prisoners.

Paddy, on the last day at sea, called me to his bed and asked me if I wanted to know what happened to his Korean guard the day word spread around the camp like a firestorm that American paratroops were coming down from the sky to save them. I nodded, and he began . . .

"Whin we heard we wuz bein' freed yez could hear yellin' all around the mine. Oi laid me bloody shovel down and took a look at me guard. He began backin' away f'm me, and oi knew phwat oi would do. Oi folleyed him until he backed into the coal face. His eyes looked loike the pig he wuz, as I reached and grabbed his sword from the scabbard . . . thin oi measured him off and oi yelled, 'yez cruel little sonofabitch, take this f'm me!' and oi cut his head off clean wid the top of his shoulders."

That explained the dried blood on the sword Paddy had brought back and the Jap flag wrapped around it.

Paddy Parks and others like him tried their war criminals summarily and then executed their own sentences. It was not the finest hour of the Anglo-American legal system, but it probably saved the necessity for holding a lot of expensive trials.

I never saw or heard from Paddy after he left the ship at Southampton, but I often wondered . . .

The short-legged ones

Some men were reticent about their treatment during captivity. But others were eager to show you their injuries and tell you how they had come about. These men seemed to want to make a record, to tell the story so that it could not be glossed over later. One short-legged man asked if I wanted to know how his legs had gotten uneven. I had seen so many of these men on the ship, walking as if they were on a hillside, of course I was curious and interested and wanted to hear his story.

We went into the OR and he disrobed to show me his leg, and told me that what had happened to him was a common method the Japanese and Korean guards used for punishing prisoners, but particularly those men who tried to escape: the guards would fire a bullet at the ileum about midway between the spine and the hip socket. The steel jacketed 25-caliber bullet would shatter the bone, so if the victim lived, and the bone knit, the one leg would always remain shorter than the other.

General Wainwright

One man in the ward told me the same story over and over again. I can't vouch for its authenticity, but it had affected him deeply, and he needed to tell it.

He said he was in the same camp with many Americans from Corregidor, including General Wainwright. He said once he saw General Wainwright venture over the line along the barbed wire fence and stand looking mutely off into the distance. A guard came storming up to him screaming in Japanese or Korean. The general either didn't hear, or didn't comprehend. So the guard took his square club and whacked him across the temple and cheek bone. The blow knocked the general sprawling in the dust, and he tried to get up, but couldn't find the strength. So he crawled over to the fence and hooked bony fingers into the strands of wire and slowly dragged his emaciated body to a standing position of attention. The guard went berserk with rage, and beat him again and again with the club, long after the general was prostrate on the ground, probably unconscious.

I remembered, then, sitting in a darkened movie house in New York a few months before and watching a newsreel of the Japanese surrender. It was held on the *U.S.S. Missouri* in Tokyo Bay on September 2, 1945. Wainwright and his British counterpart, General Percival, had put on a few pounds since their liberation a few weeks earlier, but they didn't begin to fill out the uniforms they were wearing. I recalled the appearance of the two men as they stood looking over Douglas MacArthur's shoulder, as he was seated at the desk signing the document of unconditional surrender. Their faces were gaunt and bruised, with skin drawn tight over the skulls, and eyes sunk deep in hollowed-out sockets. General Wainwright's bruises could have been caused by a square club striking the side of the face just below the temple area ...

The English doctor

Now and then some of the prisoners would talk about a doctor who had been imprisoned with them at a camp where the prisoners had been used as slave labor to build railroads and bridges. They all seemed to have incurred a deep respect and affection for this man. About the third day out, one of the short-legged men came into the hospital carrying a worn and badly-stained small wooden box. He said it belonged to their doctor. He opened it to show me the contents.

" 'e wanted you to see wot he did 'is bloomin' surgery wiv."

I saw bits of scrap metal shaped like probes, pieces of torn metal with honed edges, and a decrepit pair of needle nose pliers. That was all. And with these improvised tools he had managed to lance infected sores, remove bullets, set bones, suture wounds . . .

I wanted so much to meet this man and talk with him.

I asked the short-legged fellow if he wouldn't take John Bobb and me to meet the doctor, but he shook his head sadly.

" 'E sent word to you blokes 'e's doin' all right. Not to worry, but tyke good care of his men, 'e said . . . 'e's dyin' 'imself, don't y' know."

And then finally, England! Even the empty faces of the mentally disturbed seemed to light up with some glimmer of anticipated joy. The men who were able to stand crowded the deck rails for their first look at England as we entered the Southampton harbor and docked.

We were busy in the hospital getting some of the non-ambulatory patients ready to debark, when I heard excited voices outside saying, "They're 'avin' 'im greeted by 'er Majesty down at the gangplank."

I wanted to see what was going on, so I edged my way through the crowd of men into an empty place on the rail on the starboard side of Boat Deck. As I was turning to look I saw a woman in a white hat far below bending over a man on a litter. I saw her pin something on his chest as she was talking to him. The men around me were all crying openly. It was an emotional moment for all of us, and I found myself weeping too.

I turned to the fellow next to me and asked him who the man was, and what medal had been bestowed.

"That's our doc," he replied proudly. "I dunno for sure, but it sounded to me like the 'Vicky' itself."

The Victoria Cross! That was the big one. ..almost as big as the legend of the man who received it that day.

So then, one by one, the former prisoners disembarked, some walking, some carried on litters. I couldn't help but wonder how they were going to cope with the austerity of this post-war

England they were coming home to. We had never quite been able to satisfy the belly hunger of the 201 patients we had in the troop hospital. Now they were returning to a country where food shortages were critical, and in which individual tragedies were the commonplace and accepted fact. What kind of future lay in store for these men who had suffered so much?

Above: *Signal flags — don't ask me, I don't read.*

Upper left: *Bow of* Queen Mary, Southampton Pier.

Lower left: *Royal guards greet our arrival.*

Chapter 9

HIGH FINANCE

The T-O

Moonlighting had to become a way of life for many of us because our monthly stipend was far from munificent, and we had families at home to support. There was something sinister called "Tables of Organization," which always seemed to put the whammy on any reasonable request for an increase in rank and therefore in pay.

The T-O dictated that there should be one first sergeant, one tech sergeant, a couple of buck sergeants, and a limited number of corporals in an outfit, no more, no less. So no matter how deserving, until there was a vacant spot in the T-O, merit could not be rewarded by anything more than a pat on the back.

There was a requirement at the Brooklyn Army Base Terminal of the Transportation Corps to which we were attached that paper shufflers with so many stripes on their sleeves had to leave their desk jobs at least once every six months for foreign duty of some sort. A quick round trip to Europe on the *Queen* fulfilled this requirement and made a pleasant vacation besides. But the travelling non-coms and officers had to be temporarily assigned to our unit in order to qualify as being on "foreign" service. Hence these temporaries customarily filled up our medic's T-O and managed to have a nice sea voyage

157

while saving their stripes. But by filling our T-O they cancelled out our chances of promotion and an increase in pay.

I guess we wouldn't have minded if these "temporaries" had been willing to work, because we always needed extra hands. But they weren't . . . they weren't, that is, until Major Freund decided to lower the boom.

"If they are taking up our T-O," he said, "then they work. Offer them a broom or a swab, and if they refuse, report it to me and I'll handle it."

And with customary thoroughness, handle it he did. Those of us who were still privates had the great pleasure of telling master sergeants where to go and what to do. But the pleasure was short-lived, because all of a sudden it was as though bubonic plague was epidemic on the *Queen Mary*. The Base picked more receptive waters on which to float their elite corps of desk jockeys back and forth across the Atlantic, and some of us got the upgrades in rank to which we were entitled.

Moonlighting

Across the Hudson River opposite the Cunard Pier was a place called the Weehawken Docks, owned by the New York Central Railroad. Any time we were in port and desperate for cash we could sign on with the NYC as surrogate longshoremen. After duty hours, we'd grab the Weehawken Ferry, which was free to servicemen, and check in at what they called the "shape up" shack. Usually there was some sort of food or drink available which the New Jersey longshoremen had "rescued" from the contents of damaged crates.

The first time I worked the docks I wasn't quite sure what perks our temporary status entitled us to. When I saw my fellow workers take time off to dine on some Russian borscht (made in Chicago) and Canadian beer, I stood at a distance and waited for them to finish. I must have looked like the poor boy standing outside the candy store window, because a foreman with a nose that ran amuck across his face came out to where I was standing and shoved a liter of beer into my midsection.

"Here, soldier," he bellowed, "when one longshoreman drinks, they all drink."

And I don't really care for borscht, but I sure did enjoy that Saskatchewan sarsaparilla.

On troopships, of course, alcoholic beverages were strictly taboo. That same night two other medics from the *Queen* named Britt and Bloom, who were also working the docks, decided to smuggle twelve liters of that good Canadian beer aboard the ship. One of the regular longshoremen helped them load the bottles into Britt's fatigue jacket, and the two of them quit early and strugggled with their contraband across the maze of railroad tracks and between the boxcars, carrying the makeshift cargo sling between them. Just as they passed under one of the big light towers that illumined the yards a railroad guard stepped out of the shadows, and I thought for sure they would be apprehended and charged with grand larceny. But the guard's attention was momentarily diverted by a cheer from the longshoremen. The foreman had announced that our remaining work was in the category of "git it and go!" To the men this meant, finish the mountain of freight and go home with full pay; and men, who minutes before had been handling cargo with the enthusiasm of pallbearers, suddenly fell to and got five hours work done in three.

While the guard was looking the other way Britt and Bloom managed to pass back into the shadows, and from the shadows to the ferry dock, and thence on to the ferry where they could sit down for a few minutes and plan their strategy for getting past the MP's who guarded the *Queen's* gangplank.

I spent the next several hours while I was transporting crates from the dock to waiting railroad cars worrying about Britt and Bloom, and contemplating their fate. Finally I picked up my cash pay and hustled back to the *Queen* where I found a party well under way on D Deck. Britt and Bloom were grinning from ear to ear, and were glad to satisfy my curiosity about the sequence of events.

It seems they had indulged in a nip or two on the ferry to fortify themselves for the hard walk ahead, and to make up for having failed to come up with a viable plan of action. They left the ferry and started up 12th Avenue towards Pier 90, struggling under the great weight of the cargo sling. But about a block away from the ship they again felt the need to refuel, and sat down on the curb of 12th Avenue, utterly dejected at the prospect, on the one hand of giving up their cherished booty, and on the other, of the disciplinary action they would be subject to when the MPs looked into the makeshift cargo carrier.

A Navy shore patrol in a Navy Carryall vehicle stopped to see what was the matter, and the Chief Petty Officer in charge soon got the whole story out of them.

Perhaps the Navy in the form of one CPO decided to scuttle Army discipline; perhaps the CPO was a kindred spirit whose stripes camouflaged a pure heart; perhaps the CPO just had some very thirsty fellows under his command. In any case, it was "Bring your cargo, boys, hop in. We'll have a shot at it. We haven't done anything for the Army lately."

And so reinforced, Britt and Bloom and their husky newfound friends converged on the aft gangplank and made a successful invasion of the *Queen*. And although the Navy shore patrolmen steadfastly maintained that their rules absolutely forbade any drinking on duty, they were obviously responding to a rule of a higher order in lifting their glasses in joint toasts in our quarters that afternoon. Come to think of it, this may well have been the humble beginnings of a policy which was later adopted by the Joint Chiefs in principle, if never quite in practice: the unification of the armed services.

Funny laundry

A friend we called "Sarge," who shall otherwise remain nameless, was a classic example of that kind of Yankee ingenuity we associate with free enterprise wherever we find it.

There was not much in the way of luxury items in England in those days immediately following the war, and many items which would ordinarily be considered necessities were equally hard to come by. A case in point was alcohol: spirits to clean out rusty pipes were particularly scarce. Sarge, who hailed from north central Ohio, developed a close friendship with an English pubkeeper, who wondered if Sarge had any ideas for a solution to this economic conundrum which would assure the pubkeeper of a steady supply of whisky to sell.

Sarge gave the matter his earnest attention. His first step was to check things out around the *Queen Mary*: the cargo net, the various types of supplies which were taken aboard, the labeling of different items, the methods of handling specific types of cargo, the disposition of supplies after they were on the ship, etc.; and his research indicated that the hospital laundry constituted a fertile area for more intensive investigation and planning.

On his next trip home Sarge found a source for the brand-name products which his English friend wished to sell, a source able to provide the various brands in sufficient quantities to make the operation profitable. He then checked out paper merchants and made arrangements to purchase large quantities of wrapping paper which exactly matched the brown paper in which our hospital laundry was wrapped when it was delivered from the Brooklyn Army base.

His next move required some finesse, but did not prove to be as difficult as Sarge anticipated. Joe was the reliable truck driver who picked up our Army's supplies at the Brooklyn base and delivered them to the ship. For the nominal consideration of $10.00 a trip, Joe did not find it too much out of his way to stop at the liquor store designated by Sarge and take on a load of booze, carefully wrapped in the same size packages and paper in which our laundry was usually delivered. In accordance with Sarge's instructions, he stamped all the liquor packages and all the hospital laundry "FRAGILE" to avoid any rough handling by the stevedores. Then when the cargo was delivered to the hatch area Sarge was there to sort it out. He had no problem with this—the good stuff gurgled and was a bit heavier than our bed sheets.

When we landed at Southampton, the brown paper packages labeled **"FRAGILE"** would have a further stamp on them, **"CHAPLAIN SUPPLIES,"** which I guess were buzz words guaranteed to insure careful handling by the English longshoremen.

The system worked admirably for months, but there came the time when Sarge and I were both due to be mustered out after our next round trip and the *Queen* was scheduled to go into drydock to be refitted for civilian service. Sarge came into A143 one day and sat down. I could tell he had something on his mind.

"Bob, how'd ya like to make two month's pay for maybe an hour's work this next trip?"

Gee, I made all of $78.00 a month, so I figured he was talking $150.00 an hour. Yeah, I was ready to listen.

The English pubkeeper was aware that his supplier was going out of business after the next trip, so he had given Sarge a huge last order.

Sarge explained that what he needed from me was not my fertile and creative mind, but my strong back. He had squirreled away several enormous plywood cases labelled **"PAPER TOWELS-U.S. GOVERNMENT SPECIFICATION"** so-and-so. The words **"PAPER TOWELS"** were in 5-inch letters. Sarge was taking no chances that the packages might be opened by mistake. The interiors of the crates, each large enough to contain a refrigerator, he had carefully padded and filled with whisky cartons. Aside from the fact that the cargo people might wonder why we needed so many paper towels when our troop levels had been so drastically reduced, it was an admirable solution to his problem. But I had visions of a letter to Margaret from the Army saying I had been sent to Wormwood Scrubs for an indefinite visit (Wormwood Scrubs being the British prison catering to smugglers), so I turned Sarge's proposal down. He said it was OK, not to worry, he'd find another solution.

And OK it was. As you may have gathered, Sarge was not your common, garden-variety bootlegger, he had class. I thought he would try to move those huge boxes of paper towels as soon as we hit port, so his ulcers could stop hemorrhaging. Not Sarge. We weren't due to sail west with more "war brides" and their little ones until high tide on Tuesday. On Monday he had noon chow with the rest of us, but shortly thereafter he changed clothes and donned an oversized Air Force coverall that was so big it would have fit King Kong. He smoked a cigarette, and then another. He must have been nervous, I thought. I had never seen him smoke before.

Then Sarge left the ship by the aft gang plank where the ever-alert British Customs duo held forth. We watched from port holes in A141 and A143 as he nonchalantly chatted with the Customs men. His hand motions indicated that he was describing something to them. Then he passed out of sight off the pier.

About two hours later a large Army truck with high stake sides and eight German war prisoners standing erectly in the back arrived at the pier, about fifty feet from the Customs area. Sarge got out and went over to ask the Customs men to watch the prisoners until he returned, and then he bounded up the gang plank. He was utilizing the hostility the English still felt towards the Germans to his advantage. Those Nazis bloody well better not try anything!

Sarge entered A143, and we waited in silence.

"What's goin' on now?" he asked.

"I see two British Customs men staring hard at eight German POWs like they wished one of them would make a crooked move," I replied.

He lit another cigarette and announced to the assembled company what he had discovered the day before, that the ship's elevators were too small to handle his packing cases. That helped to explain the eight stalwart German prisoners he had handpicked for the job. When he finished the cigarette he left, walking briskly. We watched as he thanked the Customs men, and waved to the prisoners to follow him aboard.

About an hour later we watched as one prisoner came out on the narrow gangplank and turned to face the door. An end of the first crate appeared and a tug of war started. The men had to slide those heavy crates on the handrails. Fortunately the tide was in. That made it sort of downhill to the dock. I wondered if this was a factor Sarge had taken into consideration, too, when he set the time for his operation? The prisoners heaved and shoved until the crate came within range of the Customs men, who helpfully joined in and got the job done faster as a result. I held my breath. I could still make out the sign from where I watched through the porthole: **"PAPER TOWELS."** The crew loaded the first crate on the truck and then went back for another, and the process was repeated. Sarge directed the show. I wished that my photographer friend, Albert, the Royal Army Regimental Sergeant Major from the wireless room, had been aboard. What a great shot— German prisoners of war, British Customs men, and a U.S. Army Sergeant all working together in complete harmony— bootlegging!

After they had loaded all the crates Sarge passed a pack of cigarettes around, and I couldn't tell whether the British or the Germans expressed greater appreciation. Those of us who had been watching in A143 thought Sarge was a real cheapskate, and then he pushed his luck even further by once again leaving the German prisoners, the Army truck, and now the booze too, under the protection of the Customs men and returned to A143. We had scrounged up a couple of cartons of Lucky Strikes and insisted that he pass them out to his help.

Those two cartons almost cooked his goose. The Customs men were going to lay it on him because he hadn't declared them . . . sort of like the fellow who murdered a man with a pistol but only got charged with littering when the spent casing hit the grass. We noted a baleful glance in our direction from Sarge as he somehow got the matter resolved and took off in the truck with his prisoners and his booze.

Shortly after nightfall Sarge returned to the ship and to A143 where he began unloading his oversized Air Force coverall. More loose money than I had ever seen. It filled a whole dresser drawer.

A little flimflam

The Red Cross had a watering hole set up at Rainbow Corner on Piccadilly Circus in the heart of London. You could go there to get a decent sandwich and a cup of coffee for about 40¢, and sit on the second floor watching the world's busiest trading center in action. Al Draper observed the steady stream of goods being exchanged for money, and came up with an idea. On the train back to Southampton that afternoon he said he was thinking of writing his mama in Anniston, Alabama and asking her to send him an old Emerson battery-powered radio which he had used all the way through high school and for four years at the University of Alabama. He thought it might bring a good price here. What did I think of that? I didn't think much of it one way or another, but since it seemed important to him, I gave the project my blessing.

By the time we got to New York next trip the package from mama had arrived, but what a disappointment! Al and I scurried up to the operating room to analyze the reason why the Emerson didn't even put out static. Our mechanical expertise was so advanced we had the radio almost completely disassembled before I thought to ask: "Al, how old is the battery?"

A new battery did the trick, although Al was chagrined at having to make a cash investment of this magnitude. It did the trick for awhile, that is, but before we had shucked the pilot boat outside the Narrows, the Emerson quit again and stayed quit until one night, when we were about halfway across the Atlantic, and the ship was rolling about 30 degrees on the panic scale (we had this gadget on the forward bulkhead in A143 for betting purposes), the roll of the ship caused the radio to slide off a table onto the deck and suddenly the BBC came booming in from England.

What happiness! What joy! What prospects of financial success! Thereafter we treated the radio most tenderly, stowing her away among Al's underwear for the remainder of the voyage.

When we landed Al and I could hardly wait until our work area was shipshape and we were able to hustle down to Southampton Central Station for the train to London. I was going along again as a musketeer. I knew when Al hit the big time money with his Emerson, the ensuing party would be "all for one and one for all," as it had been in France.

Three little old ladies, carrying large hampers of food shared the compartment on the train with us. They were charmed by Al Draper's southern courtesy and soft Alabama drawl, and offered us some of their sandwiches and cookies. We thought we could reciprocate by entertaining them with our radio. Draper picked up the radio and twirled the knobs to find a station. Suddenly the train lurched and the "darn" radio crashed to the floor and ceased to play altogether. Except that Al didn't say "darn," he let loose a string of invectives more descriptive by far, and the little old ladies stared at him with faces expressing varying degrees of horror. This was the point at which my inborn diplomacy came into play. Al took off for the restroom, and while he was gone, in conspiratorial tones I described him to the ladies as a combat man suffering battle fatigue, doubled and redoubled. By the time I had finished I was a bit ashamed of myself. The dear old souls were dabbing at their eyes and when Al returned to his seat they looked at him as if he, and he alone, had been responsible for setting fire to Hitler's bunker.

Well, we finally got to London, and to Piccadilly, and to the Red Cross canteen, and had our customary cup of coffee at our accustomed table on the second floor at the window overlooking Rainbow Corner. Al was downcast. I wanted to help.

"Shucks, Al," says I, "it's only a case of mind over matter. Hand me that miserable piece of junk and I will demand that it play."

Al thought I had really gone bonkers by this time, but he handed that decrepit bit of useless electronics to me and I whacked it a good one with the back of my hand. "Play, you fugitive from a steel mill smelter," I said, by way of encouragement.

Well, that was too much. Whether it was the whack or the verbal abuse or the mental powers I exerted, verily, verily I say unto you, at that moment did we hear the sonorous tones of an announcer on the BBC.

Down where the action was Al attracted maybe half of the entire throng of monied consumers. The BBC was coming in several decibels higher than we should have liked, but Al let it hammer away, afraid to interfere with the production of a miracle, while the bidding went higher and higher. Finally an Arabian fellow topped it off at a fantastic £24, which was, at the current rate of exchange, the equivalent of $96.00 American. Draper was holding out for £25, when I whispered some very good advice: "For God's sake, Draper, sell it before the damn thing stops again." And realizing the value of my admonition, he gently handed the Emerson to our friend from the Middle East, and deftly plucked the pound notes from his hand.

To demonstrate my importance as an assistant in this transaction, when Draper wanted to spend some time shopping Rainbow Corner with his paper loot, I told him quick to follow me so we could "vamoose" before we got the bum's rush.

Al protested, but followed. We utilized a different entrance to the Red Cross Canteen, and five minutes had not elapsed before he appreciated the wisdom of my counsel. Looking down from the second floor window we saw the new owner of the Emerson sweep back and forth through the market area almost at a run. He was fairly short in stature, so he would leap upwards from time to time, to get an overview of the throng. It reminded me of our old dog who used to jump up like that when he chased a rabbit through a field of knee-high grass . . . the rabbit always lost the race. In this instance the Arab was shaking the radio furiously and wailing loudly in melodious syllables.

We sneaked out of London before nightfall. I thought I had earned my share of the loot. I was glad the rabbit had eluded the dog just this once.

And another flimflam

When we arrived at Southampton Central Station late that same evening, we got a ride with a cab driver named Archie, who began to question us about how often we came to England, and how many pawn shops were near the piers in New York. He said he could double any money we'd care to invest in anything made of gold, no matter the condition. Al was smart enough in the ways of the world to quiz Archie pretty thoroughly, trying to find out what his game was.

Archie said he worked for an American Air Force colonel who regularly flew to Frankfort, Germany. Gold, apparently, was a hot item in Germany. We told Archie we would think it over, and made arrangements to get in touch with him on our next trip east. It was certain we had busted our bubble in Rainbow Corner in London, insofar as any future foray into that particular marketplace was concerned.

By the time we reached New York Al and I had decided we would check old Archie out. Our decision was rather helped along by one event which occurred on that trip: I had carried a wounded patient, well wrapped in blankets, out on deck to join in a crap game one night, and had watched him count out winnings of $3,600 before I blew the whistle and carted him off to bed. It looked like there was money out there to be picked up if one had either the right connections or the right cards. Archie looked like the right connection.

So we hit the pawn shops and bought some old gold for Archie. I'll have to hand it to Al Draper. He didn't *buy* the stuff—he made them *sell* it to him. I didn't have his crust. He got a lot more for our little wad of greenbacks than I should have if the purchasing had been left to me.

Back in England again, we met Archie in the parking lot of a nightclub called "Cowherds" on the outskirts of Southampton and did, indeed, more than double our stake on the little bundle of watches and rings we had invested in. He paid off like a slot machine jackpot, and we thereupon decided that Archie was the ultimate answer to replenishing the depleted resources of impoverished Army medics.

I respected Al's business acumen, so I just let my money ride with him thereafter, and he did all the buying in New York. The next trip Archie was really pleased with the number of items we had brought, but said he was afraid the next deal might be our last because his Air Force colonel was being transferred to the Pacific. He suggested we make it a big purchase, which suited us just fine.

Back in New York Al and I blew our initial stake, all our profits, and an additional $20.00 from a couple of friends who we promised a five to four return on their investment. Al really worked the hock shops. It took three cigar boxes to hold all the stuff he bought.

Al Draper was a southerner and a gentleman. Since he was single, he said, and I was a married man with a wife and two kids, it was only appropriate that he should carry the loot-filled musette bag slung over his shoulder when we got off the ship. I carried a musette bag, too, but it was filled with a bunch of GI socks and underwear. We shouldn't have worried, though: we got the usual cheery tip of the cap from our friendly Customs men at the gangplank, before we hustled off to our pre-arranged rendezvous with Archie at the "Cowherds."

Archie was on time. He pulled his cab over to a dimly-lit corner of the parking lot, and we joined him as soon as he got out and opened the trunk. He greeted us nervously, and all the time he was sorting through our cáche of gold jewelry, he was looking over his shoulder, apprehensively. We were becoming a bit fearful, too. Archie kept fumbling with the stuff and glancing towards the back door of the nightclub, and then, suddenly, a note of sheer panic in his voice, he hissed: "Oh, my Lordy, the CID!"

In wartime England the CID was an internal security department charged with handling smuggling and similar offenses against His Majesty's government. The way Archie said it, the three letters chilled the very blood in our veins. So when Archie nodded his head in the direction of the side door of the "Cowherds" where a man in a trench coat and felt hat stood smoking a cigarette, there was nothing we wanted more at that moment than to vacate the premises and get lost in the fog. Archie whispered a time and place to meet him to collect our money, and drove off. We didn't want to appear precipitate in our actions, so we waited a few moments, trying to look as though we were engaged in casual conversation. The CID man finished his cigarette and returned to the nightclub, and Al and I stood there, both of us realizing at the same moment that we had probably been flimflammed by a real con artist.

With diminishing expectations we went the next evening at the time Archie had specified to the place Archie had specified, but what we had surmised proved only too true. We wasted a lot of hours the next few days and the next few trips looking at Southampton cab drivers, searching for one in particular. We visited the office of the cab company and learned they had thirty drivers, but no one named "Archie." Finally, we accepted the inevitable.

I guess it was only what we had coming after the Emerson radio episode.

Chapter 10

ROUND TRIP

Bury him where the tulips grow

It was the first week in March, 1946, and with the consummate logic of the Army, after traveling with a reduced complement of medics when we had a shipload of wounded, now, headed back to Southampton with no wounded, we were suddenly given not only a Transport Surgeon but also a contingent of twenty WAC nurses. Forget the incongruity of it, we old timers were determined to take full advantage of our new-found leisure, and let the WACs take the brunt of the workload from then on.

I had two ideas for using my time. I wanted to do a little more exploring around my favorite ship; and, after a three-day, 1,200 mile weekend, traveling via the thumb, I was dead tired and ready for lots of hours in the sack.

As we were preparing to sail, I got a call over the public address system directing me to meet an ambulance at dockside. The ambulance contained a patient from the Saranac Lake Tuberculosis Hospital. He was a former officer of the Dutch Navy who had become seriously ill a couple of years before while his ship was docked in New York Harbor, and after the disease was diagnosed he was sent to Saranac Lake, where he had spent the intervening years. According to the attendant, the man was dying, and his one wish was to be able to die on the soil of his homeland. The attendant said the staff at Saranac had become very fond of the Dutchman, and hoped we would give him the best possible chance of realizing his wish.

I assured the attendant we would, but when I had an opportunity to examine the patient and look at his records I realized it wasn't going to be an easily-kept commitment: it would be simply a race against time to keep the man alive for the five days which the crossing took, now that the war was over and we could sail without zigzagging.

Major Freund had gotten his discharge one trip earlier. Our new Transport Surgeon was Captain Carl Glienke of Wisconsin. After Sergeant Reilly's departure we had closed the isolation hospital deep down in the bowels of the ship, so Captain Glienke decided to put the tuberculosis patient in the farthest room of the Troop Hospital, as distant as possible from the other patients. But to protect the nurses and other patients from contamination, he laid down some precautionary guidelines with respect to wearing masks and gowns and gloves, and about sterilizing equipment.

The dying man's lungs were so far gone, he had trouble speaking more than a word or two at a time, and the few words he tried to say were difficult to understand because he had never become fluent in English, and none of us understood Dutch. Nevertheless, his eyes were very expressive, he was a gentle man, and we all found ourselves becoming more and more personally involved in the project of keeping him alive on this trip across the ocean.

But, as I said, with our additional help, I spent less time in the hospital than I ever had before, so I didn't see a great deal of him early on. He needed oxygen frequently, and he needed a lot of competent nursing, and the WAC medics took marvelous care of him. I often thought wistfully how wonderful it would have been to have had them with us on some of our earlier voyages when the pace was so frenetic.

One afternoon I had laid down on my bunk in A143, fully clothed except for my shoes, intending to read, but instead fell fast asleep. Suddenly I was awakened by WAC First Sergeant Lynn Durkin who was screaming and beating on my door.

"The Dutch officer is dying!"

I didn't wait to put on my shoes but ran back with her to the Troop Hospital, and down the length of the hospital to the patient's room at the far end, thankful that, whatever the emergency, he wasn't shut away down in the old isolation ward which was so remote and inaccessible.

Lynn was right. When I got there our patient was clutching the coil springs of the underside of the bed above his, using fingers so emaciated they looked like talons. He had suffered a spasm of the diaphragm, which caused his lungs to separate from the abdominal viscera, and his belly had forced itself up to the top of the rib cage, leaving a deep cavity where his abdominal organs should have been. There was no facial mask: his eyes bulged from their sockets and the mouth was open wide. If there was any visible sign of breathing I couldn't discern it; and there certainly wasn't time to take a pulse.

I knelt down beside him and grabbed for the oxygen apparatus, but to my horror the mask was gone! The nurse had taken it to be sterilized, and I had only the oxygen tube and the valve on top of the tank to work with.

I began the precarious valving of oxygen through the tube, trying to substitute my oversized hand for the oxygen mask, holding the tube between my fingers, and the hand itself over the open mouth. But just filling him with oxygen wasn't going to do any good if we couldn't get it down into his lungs. To accomplish this I needed to counteract the effect of the spasm by putting enough pressure on his chest to force the diaphragm downward. But it was a risky trade-off: Captain Glienke had earlier described the Dutchman's lung tissue as resembling wet cardboard. Too much pressure, and the lungs would rupture resulting in instant death; too little pressure, and the diaphragm would continue to block the lungs, the lungs would not get enough oxygen to maintain life, and the patient would die. I said a little prayer and tried to work gently and rhythmically, using one hand to hold the oxygen tube and the other to press downward on the diaphragm, pressing and releasing, pressing and releasing.

After a few minutes I felt someone putting a cotton mask over my nose and mouth. It was Marie German, a very fine WAC nurse who hailed from Penn Yan, New York. With her customary thoughtfulness and care for others, she was trying to keep me from getting a big charge of tuberculosis germs from the patient.

It seemed like minutes, but it was well over an hour that I knelt there beside his bed. Slowly, slowly the belly muscles relaxed, slowly the facial color changed from a deeper blue to a lighter blue and then back to the grayish pallor which was his ordinary skin tone. The face took on the mask of life again. He began to breathe on his own, first in shortened gasps and then with more regularity.

Miraculously, he was going to make it. Miraculously, the lungs had not ruptured. I was suddenly very, very tired, but when I tried to rise, my knees were trembling, and I had to catch at the edge of the bed for support and stand still for a moment until strength returned. He couldn't turn his head, but he reached out with his claw of a hand to clutch at my hand in silent gratitude.

Thereafter, and until we docked at Southampton, I stayed pretty close to his room. When he was carried from the boat on a stretcher the WAC medics were all lined up to say goodbye. I waited my turn, and then gave him a military salute. He nodded gently and raised a beckoning finger. I saw he was trying to speak, so I knelt down beside him.

His words came haltingly, in hoarse whispers.

"Danks .. to you . . . I die . . . in . . . Holland."

I tried to say something appropriate, but could only nod in response. I was too choked up to speak.

We never heard whether he made it back to Holland, but none of us ever doubted that he did.

Sawdust and oxygen

Maintaining the Dutch officer took a heavy toll on our supply of oxygen, so as soon as we got into Southampton Al Shriner, our supply sergeant, requisitioned a re-supply from the 14th Port.

We were due to sail in twenty-four hours, and we still hadn't gotten the oxygen and we still hadn't loaded any troops. A familiar face from the engine room crew popped into the Troop Hospital and said, "Hey, matey, wot in 'ell is all those women and little nippers doin' comin' aboard?'

"Oh, probably a guided tour, don't you suppose?"

"One 'ell of a tour it is, then," he replied. "They's 'underds of 'em, all carryin' jibbety bags and the like . . . and wot's more, the cargo slings just brought in tons of sawdust in 'underd pound bags. Wot do you make of that, matey, eh?"

"Sawdust!" I exclaimed. "What in the world do we need sawdust for?"

"Demned if I know," he snorted, and left.

But I soon found out. My "guided tour" constituted our passenger list: thousands of war brides and children.

Then suddenly I became concerned. I knew the hospital had not been supplied with anything unusual, and I was not trained to know what supplies we would need to care for sick women and little one and two-year old children. I tried to find Captain Glienke to discuss it with him, but he was unavailable. The WAC medics were still ashore, and Al Shriner and Si Amkraut, the laboratory technician, were the only officialdom at hand.

Shriner went to check again on the oxygen we had requisitioned, but it had not arrived. I told him he'd better get ashore and see to that, at least. Shortly after he left Nurse Captain Longanecker, the WAC officer in charge, came aboard. She did not seem at all surprised about our passenger complement: apparently she had prior knowledge. It was just "us old boys" who hadn't gotten the word.

I asked her if we had everything we would need under these altered circumstances and she said, "Oh yes, I think so, if you get the oxygen."

"What about oxygen masks for little faces?" I asked.

"Oh, I'm sure we must have them on hand."

"Like hell we have! Sergeant Shriner didn't know about this change-over either, you know."

"Oh, well, then you better have him pick some up if you can get 'hold of him," she said, and walked away.

I went to the shore telephone and called 14th Port. I asked for Sgt. Moon Mullins, our friend who had always been able to deliver what we needed. If his department didn't have it, Moon could always be counted on to liberate it from another source.

A corporal answered the phone.

"Yeah, corporal, lemme speak to my Kaintuck buddy."

"Who is this?" he inquired.

"This is Copeland on the *Queen Mary*—I've got to talk to Moon, pronto."

"Then you'll have to call Kentucky, Copeland. Sgt. Mullins went home on the *Elizabeth* several weeks ago. He's probably wearin' civvies now. What can I do for you?"

"Well, I was going to ask Moon to get us some oxygen masks for little kids . . . by the way, has Sergeant Shriner been there yet to check on the oxygen we ordered?"

"Yeah, he was here. And let me set you straight. If you guys on the *Queen Mary* think everybody is going to dance a jig every time you play the violin, you got another think comin'."

He sounded like a snot-nosed brat, and I wasn't as diplomatic as I should have been.

"Listen, Corporal, this is no time for silly games. You seem to have the idea we can call the drugstore every time we run out of something in mid-ocean. We can't. We need that oxygen and the masks, and we'll be sailing in less than twenty-four hours."

But the brash young kid at the 14th Port Depot was enjoying his new-found authority, and the power to say "no" to older and wiser men. He didn't give us the masks, and he didn't give us the oxygen. Shriner went ashore again to beg a few tanks from a local Southampton Hospital, but he couldn't cut through the red tape—such are the advantages of peacetime. So when the big horns on the *Queen Mary* blew long and loud, and tearful, middle-aged parents waved farewell to their war bride daughters and grandchildren, the gangplanks came away and we sailed for New York, long on sawdust, short on oxygen.

If the powers-that-be in the Supply Department were not knowledgeable about the requirements of a shipboard hospital, they certainly were right on target with the sawdust. When the war brides and their little tots who had been subsisting on the austerity diet of wartime and post-war England began eating the richer foods supplied by the *Queen Mary*, it played havoc with their digestive tracts. Add to this the bumps and grinds of the *Queen* as she hit the ground swells off Land's End, well, it would have taken an army of stewards to keep up with the vomiting that soiled the decks and corridors of the *Queen* on that voyage. The sawdust was our life-saver that trip.

It was the middle of March and the seas were rough and the winds were cold and bitter. The Troop Hospital began filling up. My worst fears were realized when a child wracked with pneumonia needed oxygen to assist her breathing. We had only one cylinder of the precious gas left, and about three more days at sea. We had only adult-sized oxygen tents on hand, which would have wasted our limited supply unnecessarily, so I improvised a small enclosure with X-ray film windows which would be adequate for the child but conserve our dwindling supply. Then another little tyke developed breathing problems, and I made another tent for her. I spent part of that night on the deck in between the two little girls, valving the oxygen off until they got restless, then turning it on again for a short time.

But even these economy measures were still using up our supply at an alarming rate. As soon as the ship came to life the next morning I sought out the Chief Steward and told him our

Above: *War brides leaving England.*
Right: *The Nursery*
Below: *The Mess Hall set up for war brides and children.*

Stuffed animals for our children.

problem. He and I had a mutual liking and respect dating back to the time of the Henri episode, the little Belgian stowaway.

I wondered if there was any oxygen on the ship in the event our supply was exhausted. He promised to check and get back to me.

Within the hour he rang me up to say that there was one, and only one, cylinder of oxygen on board, a cylinder used for welding which had already been partially used. He said we could have it if—and only if—it was a matter of life and death, because there was just as much chance of needing it for an emergency welding job.

I notified the Transport Surgeon and the newly-commissioned young doctor who had been assigned to us in England. Someone wondered whether welding oxygen could be used on human beings. I said I certainly didn't know, but suggested they ask the bridge to radio the Boston Navy Center and get an opinion.

The answer came back shortly: "Oxygen is oxygen; make the usual use of it." That relieved some of my anxiety and I slept more soundly that night.

The baby who stopped a Queen at sea

The morning of March 16, 1946 Si Amkraut brought me something to eat from the mess, and sat down to talk while I was eating and getting dressed. In the course of the conversation he mentioned there was a woman in the hospital who had started labor pains, but the new doctor had put her on some unnamed drug to hold off the main event. I told him to keep his fingers crossed, because it would be a premature baby, since none of the war brides was supposed to be past the fifth month of pregnancy. The news left me a little apprehensive.

Si had no sooner left than WAC Captain Longanecker popped in and asked, "Sergeant, do we have a baby incubator?"

"No."

"Well, I may as well tell you, we're going to have a premature baby on our hands real soon," she said, her voice betraying her anxiety.

"Why in the world didn't someone tell us old hands what this trip was going to involve?" It was a rhetorical question, I didn't expect an answer and I shouldn't have asked it, except that I was so angry.

"By the way, is Captain Glienke experienced at delivering babies," I asked, "or do we have to depend on the new young doctor?"

"I'm not sure just what either of them can do," she said, "And it's been a long time since I worked in obstetrics."

"Oh, my God!" It was as much a prayer as an expletive.

"One thing . . . all of us are depending on you to come up with an incubator, somehow, someway."

Nurse Longanecker had her hand on the doorknob and was ready to leave.

"Hold on a minute," I said. "Is the general idea of an incubator to provide an environment as near like the mother's womb as possible?"

"You got it," she said, and left.

I was dog-tired from being up all night with the two little girls, and thoroughly disgusted at the mess we were in, but the situation called for immediate action. I ran out, and almost collided with one of the ship's engineers.

"Where in hell is the ship's carpenter shop?"

He gave me directions.

I had not laid eyes on the old gentleman who doubled as Ship's Carpenter since the days of "Fireball Rose', when my unleashed GOE anaesthesia machine had torn off the operating room doors, and he had shown up to make repairs. We had both made every subsequent crossing with the *Queen*, but because of the vastness of the ship, we had not encountered each other again.

I told him our problem, and described what I had in mind, a box of a certain size with a cover, several apertures for oxygen and other purposes, and an opening for a window in the lid. As

I was talking he was selecting some beautiful pieces of white pine about twelve inches in width.

I couldn't be of any real assistance to him, so I hurried back to the hospital. The WAC medics were all busy, and it seemed ominous to me that the operating room doors were closed.

One of the WACs told me the oxygen tank gauge was getting low, so I decided it was time to call the Chief Steward to line up the welding tank oxygen he had promised. In no time at all, a crewman trundled in the tank, and I immediately checked the gauge. Old lady Fate was playing fast and loose with us again. The welding tank had only a little more oxygen than our own badly depleted tank. Even so, I had the crewman switch tanks and leave ours in reserve—I was thinking about that welding emergency the Chief Steward had mentioned.

Then I got the softest clean Army blanket I could find, a clean sheet, a pair of bandage scissors, and some X-ray film, and ran back to the carpenter shop. It had been less than two hours, but the old gentleman had already finished putting the box together and was busy sanding off the rough edges. When this was done he fitted the X-ray film to the aperture left for a window and helped me line the bottom and sides of the interior with the blanketing and sheeting which we cut to fit.

Then he hustled off and got the ship's electrician who fitted a light socket attached to an electric cord to a hole we had left in the lid of the box for that purpose.

I thanked them both and hurried back to the Troop Hospital with the makeshift incubator. Amkraut came out of the laboratory and helped me set up a table near an electrical outlet, and while we were trying to find the right wattage bulb, a distraught group of WACs, headed by Chief Nurse Longanecker, brought out a little three and one-half pound baby boy, wrapped in a blanket.

I lifted the lid from the pine-box incubator, and the nurse carefully and tenderly placed the baby inside. Although I had been with my wife when both of our sons were born, I wasn't prepared for this. Our sons were full-term. This little boy seemed tiny beyond belief.

I watched with growing anxiety as Nurse Longanecker tried to make the little fellow comfortable. It seemed as if he were trying to bite at the air. Nurse Longanecker turned to me abruptly and said, "Take over here. I'm supposed to get back in there to help the doctor!"

The little fellow had now become my responsibility, but there was nothing in my background or experience to guide me. I worried more and more over those biting movements, particularly since there were no crying sounds. Amkraut was hovering on the the other side of the incubator, equally concerned. I asked him to get Captain Glienke and the new doctor—perhaps this was within their competence. He went into the surgery, but quickly reappeared.

"They're busy, but will come when they can," he said.

"Si, take a look at his color . . . do you think he's getting cyanotic?" I asked.

"He sure as hell is!" Amkraut agreed.

"Look, Si, run get that cylinder of oxygen and get it in here pronto!"

Si returned almost immediately with our badly depleted tank and a length of hose, but of course, no mask of any kind, we didn't have any.

In the meantime I had plugged in a vaporizer unit—the same unit that set fire to the draperies in Colonel Richards' bedroom—and ran the hose from the vaporizer through a hole we had left in the side of the box for that purpose. Then I closed the lid and started valving oxygen into the makeshift incubator very slowly while we watched through the X-ray film window in the top.

Three things soon became obvious: one, the oxygen would soon be gone if used in this manner; two, the therapy wasn't helping the little fellow; and three, we needed a doctor to tell us what was going on and what to do about it.

"Si, have you got anything in the lab we could use to improvise a face mask?" I asked.

Si was not only a competent lab tech, he was also a good soldier. He didn't drag his feet, he moved.

One of the things he returned with was a small glass funnel. I grabbed it and placed it in an inverted position over the tiny baby's nose and mouth. It fit quite well. And the pipe fit the oxygen hose nicely. We were in business for the moment.

I tightened the valve on the oxygen tank to lessen the flow, and then suddenly felt all my physical strength ebbing away. It had been a long time since I'd had any rest. Amkraut relieved me, and the long ordeal of hand administering oxygen began. I slumped over on a small mountain of clean Army blankets and instantly fell asleep.

But the tensions of the past few days peopled my sleep with carpenters sawing in dark pine forests, faceless doctors and nurses carrying kangaroo joeys, and oxygen tanks with large **"EMPTY"** signs painted all over them.

Amkraut shook me awake. I had slept just ten minutes, but the blueness of the baby's face had abated during my brief rest, and he seemed to be sleeping. Si said his arm was developing a cramp, so I relieved him. Moments later, my good friend, Slim, the Chief Master-at-Arms (the ship's fireman-policeman), appeared at the entrance to the ward.

" 'ow's it goin', Sarge?" he asked.

"Slim, we've got one helluva problem. I got the oxygen tank from the welding shop, but we're still going to run out. How long until we make Pier 90?"

"Oi'd say at least thirty-six hours, mebbee an hour more, an hour less," he said.

I must have stayed silent for a long time. I was trying to calculate the fate of the two little girls with pneumonia, and the preemie, the length of time our supply would last in relation to the need. The situation looked desperate. I certainly didn't want to be the one to make the decision when it was a question of priority among the three children, or any others who developed problems in the meantime. Slim's next words just barely penetrated my consciousness.

"Sarge ... you know 'oi have an oxygen supply ... on'y oi 'ave me 'ands tied ... it's the backpacks wot we use in fightin' fire and the loike, in enclosed spyces." He spoke haltingly, as if it were costing him a good deal to make this revelation.

"Slim, you may be our last resort!"

"Sarge, Oi'm an old mon. Y' wouldn't want to see me sacked, would 'ye?"

"I understand, Slim. Only in a world that has consisted of nothing but death and destruction for so long, here is a little life we may be able to save."

It was dirty pool to use this kind of rhetoric on a Cunard officer. Cunard requires a strict adherence to regulations, and suffers no exceptions—but I thought the situation warranted the strategy. And it worked.

Slim had no sooner departed, than the young doctor put in a rather tentative appearance. I began to demonstrate the curious activity of the baby when direct application of oxygen was interrupted. Then I made a serious blunder. I had been accustomed to working with Major Freund, who always appreciated information and suggestions if they were made in the interest of the patient. So when I suggested that the baby might be fighting for air because not all the mucous membrane had been cleared from the air passage, the young doctor thought his professional skill was being challenged.

I then managed to compound the error: I asked him directly if he had held the baby in an inverted position and given it a slap on the buttocks to cause the mucous to be emitted from the mouth. I had seen Dr. Hade do that to each of my sons immediately following birth.

The young doctor's tone was sarcastic.

"Of course not, Sergeant, you must be very old-fashioned. That isn't done anymore. I used a small tube and sucked the mucous out."

"Well," I said, digging the hole even deeper, "I am almost positive there is some of the mucous still in there. I listened to his chest as best I could with the stethoscope, and I heard a kind of high-pitched whistling sound when he inspires. Won't you please just use the old procedure as a favor to me before the mucous hardens?" I pleaded.

"Since when do enlisted men go around with stethoscopes checking up on doctors' work?" he growled. And now he was truly adamant. "No, I will not indulge you in your little whims."

I saw the battle was lost. He talked of having sick people to look after, and departed.

I looked at Amkraut and he looked at me.

"Go ahead and do it, Bob" he said.

"Do what?"

"Go ahead and pick this baby up by the feet and smack its little bottom before it's too late. I think you're right."

"Suppose I am right," I said, trying to foresee consequences. "Suppose I dislodge the mucous and then the little fellow chokes to death without a medical officer here?"

I was desperate. I felt a hollow pain in my stomach. "Tell you what," I finally said, "you go see if you can find Captain Glienke and Captain Longanecker and see if they will at least come and listen to his chest noises."

Si left to make the call, and very shortly I heard Captain Glienke being paged, and asked to report to the Troop Hospital. In the meantime Si returned with Captain Longanecker in tow.

I laid the problems out to her: we had to continuously hand-administer the oxygen via the little inverted funnel; the baby had yet to cry or make any audible sound; I had heard these unusual whistling sounds on inspiration; and we needed to figure out some way to feed the baby.

"I'm inclined to agree with you," Nurse Longanecker said. "We have some real problems here, and it's time Captain Glienke got into this. I'll keep trying to find him. Meantime, I'll send one of the WACs in with a bottle."

"Captain, send a sterile medicine dropper too. Frankly, I don't quite know how we're going to manage."

Meantime, three men in ship's uniforms arrived, each carrying a rectangular shape wrapped in a blanket under each arm. I didn't ask any questions. I just took the six "packages" one by one and hastily hid them under the large pile of Army blankets which we used to sleep on. Captain Longanecker was leaving, and saw them, but she didn't seem even remotely curious about what the crewmen were bringing in to our hospital.

Then a young WAC, I think it was Angie Crusco, entered the ward bringing a baby bottle half-filled with milk and the medicine dropper I had requested. The three of us made very clumsy efforts at feeding the baby. He would gasp for air almost as soon as we put the huge nipple into his tiny mouth. Finally we resorted to the medicine dropper, one drop at a time, with an appropriate interval between drops to allow him to breathe. In about an hour we had managed to give him a whole ounce!

About that time Captain Longanecker reappeared with the Transport Surgeon. Captain Glienke was reluctant to overrule the young doctor, since he had been assigned to the *Queen Mary* for that trip precisely because he was supposed to have had obstetrical experience. Captain Glienke told the group of us what a great job we were doing, and started to leave.

At that point I stopped him to let him know how critical the oxygen supply was. I couldn't tell him about the backpacks, of course, but I did give him my estimate of how long the supply in the tanks would last at the rate we were using it for our three little patients. And it certainly wasn't going to last until we hit Pier 90.

Captain Glienke said there was no chance of taking either of the little girls off oxygen. The one with the bad cough was not doing well at all, he said. There was even reason to believe she might require an appendectomy.

So there it was, the end of the line: all three children needed the oxygen, the oxygen supply was due to run out in a couple of hours, and thereafter we would be wholly dependent upon the six backpacks.

"Captain," I said, "you've got to contact the bridge and get them to get help from any ship near us that has an oxygen supply. And see if they will tell you how far we are from a U.S. Navy Base.

"What's the Navy got to do with this?" he wanted to know.

"Well, I don't think they've got anything to do with it, but I bet they'd figure out a way to help us."

I didn't realize what time it was. The windows facing aft from the ward were still covered by heavy black-out paint. In point of fact, it was nearly midnight. Amkraut and I decided to go with one-hour shifts: an hour with the hand thrust through the hole in the side of the box holding the glass funnel over the baby's nose and mouth, was a very long time. One's arm and hand and mind got very tired, and one's body cramped in numerous places.

The hour sleeping periods weren't very restful, either, but they were necessary.

About 5:00 a.m. Si shook me and gave me the bad news. Our oxygen tank was now empty. Damn, I thought, I slipped up and haven't checked on the size tubing we need to switch to one of the backpacks. But chance rolled a pair of sevens, and our hose fit perfectly. I kept the contraband tank hidden under the Army blankets with only the hose showing.

Around 9:00 a.m. the Transport Surgeon sent word that no ships had been close enough to do us any good, and he thought it would be useless to ask the Navy . . . but be sure, he said, to conserve oxygen in any way we could!

My tired mind kept saying, "you've done the best you can."

But I kept having a flashback to an incident in my childhood when I had been listening, open-mouthed and wide-eyed, to my father and Uncle Bob talking about rescue operations, and I remembered my Uncle Bob saying, "One thing about the Navy, Earl, when they cause trouble to enemies or bring help to friends, they do it quick and they do it right!"

I asked Si to hang on while I went to see how much oxygen the welding tank had on the gauge, and then I knew we were in deep trouble, even if I brought another one of the backpacks out of hiding.

I couldn't find either of our doctors, so I ignored military etiquette and went to see the Chief Steward again. He wanted to know how we were getting along, and I lost no time in getting down to business.

"Will you, my friend, do me one more, one last favor? Would you ask the bridge to put in a call to the Boston Navy Center to see if they can fly us oxygen from some base? As I understand our position, we are far past Iceland, but there must be some base within range . . . We won't hit Pier 90 until high tide tonight, right?"

"Fly!" He was dumbfounded at such an idea.

"Yes, sir. Seaplanes. I'll bet a lot of those Navy pilots are just itching to hit the sky again with some real purpose."

"But, but . . . we have a rule against stopping at sea, don't you know," he expostulated.

"I know about the rule. But there aren't any subs out there now, are there?"

"I see. Well, I'll check it out," he said.

"I knew I could count on you," I said, "more than anyone!"

I hastened back to the ward to relieve Si and his aching arm. Now I really *had* done everything I could do.

One of the WACs named Stella was making a diaper change when I re-entered, and I no more than touched Si's arm, when he dropped the funnel in the incubator beside the baby and fell down on the blankets. I could have sworn he was asleep in midair before he hit the deck.

I took over the job of administering the oxygen. Some time later our Army Chaplain, Leigh O. Wright, came in and indicated he wanted to follow the mother's wishes and christen the baby. Chaplain Wright had been on the *Q.M.* long enough for the crew to regard him as their own, so they had dubbed him "Padre".

Padre disappeared momentarily and Si woke up. We were talking about the ordeal of feeding the baby again, when Padre returned, this time accompanied by three other people, Nurse Captain Longanecker, a Red Cross lady I had seen working with the war brides, and my friend Albert, the Royal Army Regimental Sergeant Major and ship's photographer, with his camera. He was there to record the event.

Up to this time the little fellow in the incubator had been only "our baby" or "baby." Now he acquired a new identity.

The hospital pharmacy—bailiwick of Louis T. Macaronas, site of aborted party with the girls in Bob Hope's troupe.

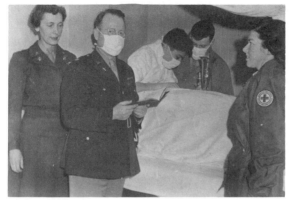

Padre christens the baby.

The Navy comes across!

Passing the oxygen tanks on board.

We learned that he was the son of Russell Smith of Coventry, Vermont, and Pauline Travers Smith, formerly of Manchester, England; he had a two year-old sister named Polly; and he was to be christened Leigh Travers Smith, Leigh after the Army Chaplain on the *Queen Mary*.

When the short, but impressive ceremony was over, Albert leaned over to me and said something which my tired brain had trouble processing.

"Just about the whole civilized world is hanging breathless on what's happening here, did you know that?"

I nodded, assenting, but I really didn't know what he was talking about. I knew the baby needed to be fed again and I had to check on the two little girls.

I went into the other room where panic was rampant. The welding tank had just hit empty. I went back into the baby's room and told Si I was going to have to take another one of the backbacks out of its hiding place. I did, but kept it well-swathed in Army blankets. Marie German regarded me curiously as I was on my knees working the Army blankets back under the bed of the little "pneumonia girl." I trundled the empty oxygen tank over so it was lying at the base of the blankets and hoped no one would notice that the hose was not connected to the oxygen tank but to something else altogether. If Marie German did notice, she didn't give a sign.

When I got up from the floor I saw the entrance doors to the hospital open slightly. It was Slim. He appeared near exhaustion. I asked if he was okay.

"A bit done-in, I am. My men and I 'ave been walkin' the ship tryin' to make sure nothin' slips up on us, y' know." He was worried about the possibility of facing an emergency without his supply of oxygen backpacks, and was taking extra precautions. This man was one of a kind!

'I'm using the first two backpacks now. Do you know how many hours we can count on from them?"

" 'ard to say, Sarge. A grown man fightin' smoke or fire would use it a bloody lot faster, I'd say." Then almost as an afterthought he blurted out, "Somethin' is cookin', though. Skipper has ordered #1 lifeboat readied for some reason."

I knew then that a minor miracle was in process of happening. I hurried back to relieve Si and told him what Slim had said. I expected him to be jubilant. Instead he looked grim.

"Bob, this little guy is getting worse all the time."

I grabbed the stethoscope and listened . . . and listened. In vain. I couldn't hear the faint high-pitched whistling sound anymore.

"Si, I know you're half dead, but will you go find Captain Glienke and tell him we're getting into more danger. I'm afraid the mucous obstruction has hardened. Also tell him we think they should alert a New York hospital, one experienced with preemies, Bellevue maybe, and ask them to meet the ship with whatever emergency equipment they have. Maybe they could even come on with the pilot boat, that'd save an hour or so."

Again, my timing mechanism was out of whack: high tide was around 7:00 p.m. New York time, someone had told me. No need to start thinking of pilot boats yet! But Si didn't seem to pick up on it, either. He left.

He had been gone quite awhile when I realized my stance was requiring less shifting from one leg to the other. Slowly my fuzzy brain caught up with this alteration in the environment. I realized the ship was stopping. I heard feet scurrying outside and excited voices in the gangway, but when I yelled out to ask, "What's happening?" no one answered. I realized suddenly that my loud voice could have penetrated the incubator, and looked down to see if the noise had bothered little Leigh Travers Smith. No. He gave no sign. I only wished to God he had.

It was an eerie feeling, this business of the *Queen Mary* being stopped dead-still in mid-ocean. But in my heart I knew what had happened. The U.S. Navy had delivered, just as Uncle Bob had said it would so many years ago. But when Amkraut came bounding in shortly thereafter, followed by seamen dressed in warm clothing and wearing life jackets, struggling with a huge oxygen tank, I was strangely apathetic.

Then I felt the turbines shaking the 81,000 tons of the *Queen Mary* back to life; I felt the rhythmic swaying of the deck underfoot, as she plowed through the seas again; and hope revived. The little eyes staring up at me from the incubator seemed oddly vacant, but I was counting on my *Queen* to make port before the life spirit drained out of the little fellow. Si relieved me again, and I ran outside to try to find someone who knew exactly where we were and when we would be docking, but instead I ran into Captain Glienke. I urged him again to request that an experienced delivery room team from a New York hospital come aboard with the pilot boat, if at all possible.

"Do you think he's that bad?" he asked.

"I really do."

"What about the oxygen delivery, wasn't that something?" he said, still excited from watching the transfer of the tank from the seaplane to the ship.

I was beginning to have more sympathy for the man. He had been thrust into this ordeal as unprepared as any of us. I had carried over from childhood my view of doctors as men with godlike qualities making infallible decisions. Dr. Glienke was a man of good intentions with a medical degree, some skills, and all the human frailties any of us have. He was also hampered by medical ethics in his relationship with the young obstetrician.

I went back and looked at my bonanza, the big oxygen tank, and wondered how I could use it in two places at once so I could quit using the backpacks. I found there was no way to recharge our depleted tank from the big one, so I called the welder. He came up with some gauges and hoses and wrenches, but he soon determined there was no simple answer.

Since the "pneumonia girl" was in a bed close to the operating room, I elected to place the big tank next to her, with a tee connector so I could run a hose into the O.R. if an emergency developed. Our baby would stay on the backpacks.

Meantime, I sneaked the backpack away from "pneumonia girl"—just in time. It had hit bottom. That pack found a temporary burial deep under the Army blankets over near the incubator. Then, with no warning at all, this warrior ran out of ammo.

I felt as if I had swallowed a "mickey finn." I mumbled something to Si about seeing if the nurse or Marie could help him, and that's all I remember. He told me later I hit the edge of the blanket pile, but the ship heaved to port and I rolled over onto the bare deck and never missed a snore.

I felt more rested this time when I was awakened. Amkraut and a WAC and Captain Longanecker were trying to feed little Leigh. Si heard me, and looked up. I could see desperation in his face. He surrendered the glass funnel to me, and shook his head sorrowfully . . . and then down he went to the pile of blankets.

Drop by painful drop the nurses fed the baby, trying to get the eye dropper in his little mouth and keep the glass funnel inverted over his mouth and nose at the same time. I told Captain Longanecker it had been hours since I had heard any whistling noise in the baby's bronchial area. She didn't answer, but her face set more sternly.

About then Albert, the British Army R.S.M. and photographer extraordinare, came in to peek at the baby. I could hear him suck in his breath in dismay. He filled me in then on what was happening in the world outside of Troop Hospital: we had been about 400 miles out when the seaplane touched down, the ship stopped, and the transfer of the oxygen tank was made; the *Queen* had since made up the time lost on her unscheduled stop; and the Captain expected to dock at high tide as usual.

The steady forward churning of the ship, running back and forth between the three children, bone-weary but with no more chance for cat-naps, frantic with worry, the hours seemed to drag endlessly, mindlessly on, and I was borne along, taken out of the warp of time altogether; but finally came the lessening of the beat of the turbines which meant we were slowing down for the pilot boat to come alongside, and my life regained its frame. I felt a surge of elation. "Quick," I yelled out to one of

192 *Warrior Without Weapons*

the nurses, "watch for some people with medical equipment looking for this baby. Don't make them wait a second!"

The *Queen* picked up a little speed so I knew the transfer had been made. Leigh Travers Smith made some spasmodic movements, and I put the stethoscope back in my ears and listened. I couldn't hear a thing! No flub-dub of the tiny heart beating. Si came in then, and I asked him to hold a pillow over my head to shut out all extraneous sounds. I listened again. Yes, there was something going on there, not the sound of a heartbeat, but a sound, nevertheless.

Si took the pillow away as I straightened up and looked at him.

"No one came on the pilot boat," he said, "except the usual quarantine officers, the pilot, and a newspaper guy with a camera. He's looking for us now. I shook him on Main Deck 11."

His face was contorted with sadness and disappointment. Victory which had seemed almost within our grasp short minutes before was going to elude us for another hour while the tugboats carefully turned the majestic ship around ninety degrees and maneuvered her into her berth.

I told Si to put a call in for the doctors to come "stat,' which was the equivalent of today's "Code Red."

The young doctor arrived first, then Captain Glienke.

Captain Glienke looked at me and said, "Pick him up, you're used to him."

I reached in the incubator and brought the little fellow out cradled in my left hand, still administering the oxygen with my right.

Captain Glienke listened carefully with his stethoscope.

"He's going . . .!" I didn't catch the rest of the sentence, but I assumed he meant the baby was going into shock.

He told the young doctor to hurry and get a syringe and coramine.

"What is coramine, Captain?" I asked.

"Heart stimulant."

"Captain, would a light stroking massage over the mediastinum help or hurt?"

C. M. Ford R.D. 'R. _____ Commander.

Towards _____ New York _____

Day of the Month _____ 14ᵗʰ March. _____ 1946.

Hells	No 1.	No 2.	REMARKS.
	2"	1'	

Wells vents lights floatouts ended
Fire appliances in readiness. Rounds by Light Officer.
Gyro error 1° H. Dev. 3½° H. Var. 22½° H. Visibility Excellent
Light breeze slight sea & swell passing clouds fine & clear.

Rounds by Night Officer

Gyro error N/u. Lat. 30° N. Dev. 3° N.
0628 Adj. Co. 260° + 2½°
mod. breeze & Sea. Slight Swell. Fine & clear.

Gyro error ½° High. Var. 19½° W Dev. 1° W. 0858 % 262° + 2°
0920 Mail & baggage spaces visited
1000 DG switched ON. 1030 Divine Service held in Main Loun...
1142 Lat ... Bank of male child & Pauline Edith Smith, British alien.
Noon Nature smooth sea fine & clear
1142 Lat 40° 52 N Long 66° 01 W Mrs Pauline Edith (passenger)
gave birth to male child (christened) Lights taken in at Sunrise A.M.
(Leigh Travers Smith)

LAT. OBD.	LONG. CHRON.	COURSE AND DIST.	VARIATION.	BEARING AND DISTANCE.
40-51 N.	66-13 W	260°, 688 mls.	18½° W	To Sun. S of Nantucket Lt 262° 156 mls / To A.C.L.V. 349 miles

P.M.
Steaming Time 25 h 00 m
Average Speed 27.52 k.

Gyro error 1° H Dev. 2° H Var. 1° W
1455 Adjusted Co 261° & a fahet., 1511 Adjusted Co 260° + 3°
Cabin smooth sea fine & clear. Visibility Excellent.
1410 Red. to 100 rpm
1421 Half Speed. 1425 Slow ahead. 1429 Stop. 1731 Slow astern. 1735 Stop. 1737 Seaplane astern landed.
1737 Away Seaboat 1743 Seaboat alongside plane & loaded oxygen. 1746 Seaboat left plane.
1755 Seaboat alongside. 1756 Seaboat left. 1802 Boat hoisted. 1805 Full ahead. 140 rpm...
1815 Signalled Calalena flyboat.
Calm Smooth Sea. Fine & clear. 20-09 N F Above ...
1838 Lat 40 30 N Long 70 5... W Leigh Travers Smith, male child of Mrs Paul... Smith (passenger) died
Gyro error ½° High Var. 13° W Dev. 1° W.

Rounds by ...

2206: Reduced to 135 rev. 2324 Red. 120 Revs.
Calm, smooth sea, 23-09 Fine & cloudy 0933 × ...
Cloudy & clear. Lights hung out at Sunset P M

Page from ship's log listing birth and death of Leigh Travers Smith (insert).

WAR BRIDE'S SON BORN ON LINER

Premature Infant Lost After Hours Despite Oxygen Aid on Queen Mary

A son born prematurely to the British wife of a former American soldier nearing New York on the liner Queen Mary died after nine hours of life despite rescue efforts that involved three Coast Guard aircraft, it became known yesterday when the ship arrived from Southampton with 2,334 war brides and children.

The infant, christened Leigh Travis Smith by Maj. Leigh O. Wright, an Army chaplain, at 2:30 o'clock Sunday afternoon, lived until 10:38 at night. He had been placed in an improvised incubator. After the ship's supply of oxygen was exhausted, more oxygen was flown to the liner by a Coast Guard seaplane. Another seaplane and a heliocopter, both operated by the Coast Guard, also flew oxygen to the ship in response to an emergency message. After they arrived it was found that the supply carried by the first plane was sufficient.

Death was the result of respiratory complications that developed while Capt. Carl F. Ghenke, an Army surgeon, and other ship's personnel labored to save the infant's life. Mrs. Pauline Edith Smith, 23 years old, mother of the child, is a native of Manchester, England.

Her husband, former S. Sgt. Russell Dow Smith of Coventry, Vt., came to Pier 90, North River, yesterday to meet her and their daughter Pauline, 2 years old. As he joined a group of about 600 men who had come to greet their wives and children, he knew nothing of the birth and death of his son. He was taken aboard the liner and informed of the details.

OXYGEN FLOWN TO AID CHILD ON QUEEN MARY

Answering an urgent request from the liner Queen Mary, inbound from Southampton, for six tanks of oxygen, a PBM plane of the Coast Guard's Air-Sea Rescue Agency sped to the vessel late yesterday afternoon and delivered the tanks fifty miles east of Nantucket Lightship.

The Queen Mary is due to dock at Pier 90, North River, at 6 A.M. today with 1,840 war brides, 600 children and other passengers, and it is believed that the oxygen was needed for a sick child. An Air-Sea Rescue unit spokesman said last night an unidentified Army officer had told him the Army would meet the vessel with an oxygen tent for an "infant litter case."

The PBM plane was dispatched from Salem, Mass., nearest Coast Guard air station to the ship. The message requesting the oxygen specified six tanks with a certain type of fitting, not available at Salem. However, the PBM took the Salem equipment, while another plane, a PBY, left from Floyd Bennett Field, Brooklyn, with the designated type.

The PBM reached the Queen Mary at 4:34 P.M. and, at about the same time, the PBY came into sight and circled the vessel. While the PBM's pilot set his ship down alongside the huge liner, the PBY remained in the vicinity until it received word from the vessel that the oxygen tanks from Salem were satisfactory. The PBY received a message of gratitude from the Mary before leaving for home.

"Can't hurt. Might help."

"You or me?" I asked.

"You!" he said.

While we were talking, almost in whispers, I heard voices in the outside corridor arguing, familiar voices and one strange one. Then someone called, "Copeland, this guy wants to take a picture. Is it all right?" and I turned around to be momentarily blinded by a flashbulb.

"Get out! I mean it!"

My tone must have been sufficiently threatening, because the door closed quickly.

I placed the baby in shock position, with feet elevated and upper torso lowered. I used my left thumb to massage gently with an upward motion over the heart, at the same time maintaining the oxygen feed with my right hand. His condition seemed to improve, and I asked the question that had been burning in my brain.

"Captain, did a call go out at all for that help from a civilian hospital?"

"Yes. I can't tell you why they weren't on that pilot boat."

Then what I had been dreading all along happened. The baby convulsed, and I saw the Transport Surgeon make a quick upward motion as he turned to take the hypodermic away from the young doctor who had just returned. I was holding the baby in my left hand, turning towards Captain Glienke so that he could administer the shot, when little Leigh Travers Smith gave up the fight . . . it was all over. I think each of us knew it then, but Captain Glienke injected the coramine into the heart with an expert thrust of the needle anyway. He kept asking me if I felt any reaction, but I shook my head. He told me to restart the massage with more vigor, and the clock ticked away. Someone came in with the news that we were being warped into the pier. No one commented. We had lost the race.

I was still mechanically massaging the heart area; Amkraut was handling the oxygen. We still hoped for a miracle.

Suddenly the doors opened and strangers came streaming into the room. Camera bulbs flashed. Confusion reigned. Our people were ordering them away, but no one was listening. Si and I were facing away from the door, and we moved back towards the pile of blankets, still working with the baby. Captain Glienke forced his way through the crowd over to us, gently shook his head and removed his stethoscope from his ears. I pulled the incubator around and laid Leigh Travers Smith down for the last time. I thought my body was going to splatter out in all directions.

A newsman with a flash camera made his way through the crowd and thrust his face into mine.

"Pick up the baby in one of your hands, again!" he demanded.

"Fella, this baby has just died. Leave him in peace."

I was crying inside. It was hard to get any words out.

"C'mon, Sarge, just one shot. No one'll know that when they see the picture!"

It was too much for my anguished soul. I snatched his camera by the straps, and if it had not been for an Army Colonel who yanked him out of my reach and forcibly ejected him, I would have hit him with all the strength I had left.

Some Army administrative officer came up and introduced himself as a Captain Rodgers, or something similar, and said I had been recommended for the Soldier's Medal. I said I didn't know anything about that, and he explained it was an award for good soldiering, not in combat. I turned to thank him, but the crowd engulfed me, and I never saw him again.

I wanted to get Slim's mostly empty backpacks returned before they were discovered, but this was no time for that, so I headed out on the Boat Deck, trying to avoid people who were pursuing me, asking all sorts of silly questions. The Colonel who had given the heave-ho to the newsman with the camera followed after me. Finally we managed to elude everyone, and standing beside the rail he introduced himself. He said he represented the Army Transportation Corps unit stationed at the Brooklyn Army Base, and that arrangements were being made for a ceremony on board the *Queen* the next day to award me the Soldier's Medal.

My thoughts were still with the baby. I was not hearing what he was saying. He must have asked a question without getting any response, because he laid a hand on my shoulder and repeated something he had said about the projected ceremony the next day which alarmed me. Would the press be there, I asked? He explained that having the press there was necessary.

We walked along the Boat Deck in silence for a while and then I said, "Colonel, suppose tomorrow in the audience there is one sharp reporter who asks the right question. What if he says, 'Sergeant, why did this happen? Why was the ship allowed to sail without an adequate oxygen supply and masks and equipment for women and children? Why were emergencies like this not foreseen? Who fouled up?' And so on, and so on. I am terribly let down and tired, sir, and I would very much like to have that medal to show my parents and my children, but I don't want to see the Medical Corps dragged around like an animal carcass before a pack of lions!"

The Colonel stopped walking abruptly and held on to the nearest lifeboat, as though the *Queen Mary* were at sea and had unaccountably changed course.

"Maybe thirty years from now the Army might want to quietly slip me a medal. But now now!"

The Colonel cleared his throat and turned and extended his hand. "Sergeant, I've been regular Army for a good many years, and thought I had seen and experienced everything the Army has to offer. But ..." Then he said a few nice things which don't bear repeating, and turned to leave.

"How do I get down off this Big Lady?" he asked.

I got him headed in the right direction and then sneaked back to the hospital by a roundabout route, still worried about the backpacks. The hospital was nearly cleared of patients, and the nurses had done a superb job of cleaning it up. I saw the hoses still in place under the pile of blankets, but the incubator was gone, and I never saw it again. I didn't know what had happened to the baby, and I tried not to think about him.[12] I began coiling oxygen hose and preparing to return those precious backpacks to the Chief Master-at-Arms when Slim himself walked in with a crew and made short shrift of it.

"Slim, I don't know what to say, or how to thank you. Too bad you can't get the Victoria Cross for risking your lifetime job."

"Not to worry, Sarge. After all, those nippers were 'alf us Britishers, don't y'know."

"I can't even sign a check showing I requisitioned them so the Army could pay Cunard back," I said.

"Righto. I'll show we 'ad some leakers," he laughed.

"A lot of leakers, Slim, a lot of leakers."

I went back to A143 and lay in the bathtub hoping to unwind. But my mind kept re-creating the events of the past four days. So I put on Class A's and went ashore. A couple of Custom's men went out of their way to be friendly, which was a real switch.

One of them said, "I hear you earned your pay this run, Sarge."

"Naw, I fouled it all up!"

And I walked out along 12th Avenue heading upriver. I never felt more alone. I didn't usually take alcohol when I was under stress or troubled, but now I wanted a good, strong drink.

Not far down the road there was a dimly-lit, waterfront saloon. I stood on the steps and peered inside. Four rough-looking dock workers were holding forth at the bar. I was startled to be addressed by a child's voice. I turned. There, in the shadows near the steps, a little boy was waiting patiently.

"Are you a soldier man?"

"Hello, little fellow, what are you doing out here this late?"

He hopped up the stairs to the glass door and pointed to one of the loud, gesturing men and said proudly: "That's my

---

12. The autopsy revealed what I had suspected—a mucous plug left in the bronchial tube and extending hair-like fibers into the alveoli of the lungs, had hardened and blocked the air passage.

daddy. My mommy sent me here to bring him home. He gets awful drunk sometimes."

The boy must have been about seven years old, just the age of my oldest son, Bobby. Suddenly, an awful longing to see my sons swept over me. I put my arm around the youngster and we walked together into the smoke-filled tavern, which smelled of stale beer, unwashed bodies, tobacco, and bathroom disinfectant. The men looked over at us, and one of them said, "Hey, kid, c'meah."

The lad obediently ran to his father.

"I want dese guys to heah how smart y'are. Tell 'em, what's ten and two, kid."

The little boy told them what ten and two was, and then, at his father's urging, went through some spelling words. The other drunks applauded, but the father said, "Hey, youse guys ain't heard nuthin' yet. Now kid, I want that you should say dat prayer the sister taught youse."

He hoisted the little boy atop the bar, and in an unbelievably sweet voice the child began to recite the Rosary:

"Hail Mary, full of grace
The Lord is with Thee,
Blessed art Thou among women,
And blessed is the fruit of Thy womb, Jesus.
Holy Mary, Mother of God, pray for us sinners
Now and at the hour of our death. Amen."

The applause was loud. "All right, Murray, all right . . . that's one swell kid. Hey, kid, you're okay."

Murray started to drink to that, when I laid my hand across his arm and forced him to turn to look at me.

"Does this little boy have a name?" I inquired softly.

"Who the hell . . ." he began, but I cut him off by a sharp squeeze on his arm.

"Okay, okay. His name is Paul Joseph. And what's that to you, buddy?"

"Murray, I'm a soldier who would like nothing better than to be with his two children tonight . . . but I can't. You can.

Now say goodnight to the bartender and take Paul Joseph
home, and surprise your wife by getting in a little earlier than
usual and a little more sober. And if I hear you call this sweet
little boy 'kid' any more, I'll lower the boom on you. Get
moving!"

As Murray and Paul Joseph were leaving I moved along the
bar to the other three men.

"Any children you should have told 'goodnight?' " I asked.

One guy wailed that his son was fifteen years old. I didn't let
him off the hook. "That's a qualifying age," I said, "you go,
too. He might like to know what you look like sober."

I sort of herded the three of them towards the door, but they
said they needed to get their jackets and "equipment." The
equipment turned out to be freight hooks, and a freight hook
can make a "fohmeedobble" weapon when applied to the
human anatomy. Somehow that didn't occur to them. They all
went out muttering about sergeants who meddled in other people's business.

"I'm going to watch you guys, and don't any of you stop till
you get home," I said. I followed them up 12th Avenue until
they parted company and went in different directions. Then I
walked back to the saloon. I felt I owed the bartender an explanation and an apology.

"Hey, Sarge, I'm wit youse on dis here ting. I get sick d'way
them bums treats der famblies. I only woik here, no skin. Say,
how's 'bout havin' one on d'house?"

But I wasn't in the mood any longer, and declined with
thanks. Still, my nerves were on edge from the events of the
past five days. I was walking down the street again aimlessly
when I saw the Weekhawken Ferry coming into the slip. I
thought of the Weehawken docks where I had worked occa-
sionally. Maybe someone I knew would be on duty there.

I recognized the collector from trips the year before. The collector kept looking at me, trying to remember why my face
looked so familiar. "Hi, soldier, long time no see. Where ya
been, whatcha been doin'?" he asked.

"Oh, nothing much," I answered, "any soldiers working tonight?"

"Hey, it *has* been a long time. Doncha know the longshoreman's union made 'em stop hiring military men?"

The collector cleared his throat and said apologetically, "Hey, sorry, but I gotta charge you for the ride now."

"Oh, I apologize. I guess I rode free too long, anyway." I laughed and handed him a nickel.

He looked at me kind of sheepishly.

"Sorry, Mac, it's a dime now," he said.

I fished in my pants pocket and found another nickel. Peace sure was hard on the budget, I thought.

I was headed for the upper deck when he called me back.

"Say, ain't youse one of them medics from the *Queen Mary?*"

I nodded.

"Now I place you . . . you used to work on the docks regular. Say, youse guys sure made news the last few days wit' that little baby and all. How's he doin'?"

"He's okay, he's with God now," I said, and suddenly I turned my back and all the sorrow and tensions of the last few days came out in great, heaving sobs.

"Oh, Jeez, I'm sorry . . . I didn't know . . . I didn't know." He patted me on the back, and when I pulled out my handkerchief to blow my nose and got control of myself and turned around again, I noticed that his eyes were filled with tears, too.

He told me to ride as long as I wanted, and I took him up on it. Finally, around midnight I thought maybe I would be able to sleep. I shook hands with the collector and thanked him, and headed back for the Gray Ghost.

Al Shriner woke me up about 9:30 the next morning. He said there was a colonel in the Troop Hospital waiting to see me.

It was the same gentleman I had guided off the ship the previous evening.

"Just wanted to be sure you felt the same way this morning as you did last night I mean about the Soldier's Medal?"

"Yes, sir, I do," I said. "I don't want any careers busted on my account. Most of the mistakes were honest ones, or at the most, stupid ones, but we'd never convince the news people, would we? And someone's neck would have to be strung in the noose. Better to let it die. Maybe in thirty years they'll offer me the medal again . . . and then I'll take it."

But thirty years have passed, and they've never offered it again. I guess I'd kind of like to have it now. It would be something to show my grandchildren and great-grandchildren.

Chapter 11

FAREWELLS

One mo' time

Most of the veterans with any length of service were discharged by February, 1946, and our group was beginning to be broken up, too. We were all eager to get home and into civilian life again, but parting with men I had spent eighteen months in very close quarters with, and been through so much with, was emotionally devastating. Some of our gang left in February and some in March, and in each case the parting was bitter-sweet. We made promises to meet again and keep in touch, but we all realized the close comradeship of those days was gone forever.

For the past year I had been taking correspondence courses at Indiana University, and had been accepted for the June, 1946 semester. I was, however, still "frozen" in station, and was beginning to get concerned about my status.

"One more trip and home you go!" This good news came from the Brooklyn Army Base via First Sergeant Lynn Durkin.

This last trip to England was uneventful except for watching the big booze operation. I made a brief visit to London to tell Nicky Brodsky goodbye, but no one was home, so I left a note in his mail slot, wishing him well, and expressing my hope that he would be successful in emigrating to the States.

I don't know whether it was by chance or design, but when we left Southampton, an impressive twin sister act took place. Beginning in the outer reaches of the Solent River and continuing all the way to Land's End, the southwest tip of England, the *Queen Mary* and the *Queen Elizabeth* sailed in tandem, side by side about one-half mile apart. I don't think this had ever happened before. When the *Elizabeth* altered course and turned north up the Irish Sea en route to John Brown's Shipyard at Glasgow, Scotland, to be re-habbed for civilian service, she gave one final ear-rending blast of her horns in farewell, which our ship acknowledged as she headed west for New York. That, too, was an emotional experience for many of us.

The return voyage was not memorable either. Oh, yes, we brought back more war brides and their little ones, but this time we were loaded for bear when it came to equipment, and we had a surfeit of staff to take care of them. The saddest part of all was seeing two war brides with two small children still waiting at Pier 90 after all the others had been joyfully reunited with their husbands; no one had come to claim them. I found out later from a corporal at the base that these two women had each married and had a child by American servicemen who already had wives on *this* side of the Atlantic, and that they would be sent back to England on the *Queen* when she departed.

The carrot and the stick

When we got to Pier 90 my orders still had not come through, so I decided to go to the Brooklyn Army Base to find out what was causing the delay. I gathered my gear and made the rounds of the ship saying my goodbyes. Then I hitched a ride to the base.

"No problem, sergeant. You'll be on your way to Camp Atterbury, Indiana, by noon tomorrow."

These words were uttered by a fellow I recognized as one of the floating paper shufflers to whom I had handed a mop some months back, when Major Freund was protecting our T-O, only now he was a master sergeant and he had opted for the regular Army. Unfortunately he recognized me, too, and I don't think his memories of our past association were especially happy ones.

I had no sooner dumped my gear on the bunk assigned to me in the huge dormitory than there was a call over the PA for Sergeant Copeland to report to Lieutenant Goodman's office.

I had come in contact with Goodman before: men were numbers to him. Therefore when I entered and started to salute I was nonplussed when this martinet of a fellow smiled and waved me to a seat.

'Sit down, Sergeant Copeland," he said, affably, "I have some good news for you."

He opened a drawer and pulled out a rolled parchment, tied with a ribbon, which he handed to me. I thought, gee, they gave me the soldier's medal after all, without a ceremony.

He continued to speak as I untied the ribbon and unrolled the parchment.

"This is your commission as a first lieutenant, Copeland. The Army Medical Corps is acknowledging your outstanding capabilities and past services."

I scanned the date and the commanding officer's signature. The thing looked real. Maybe I had misjudged this fellow.

"I don't understand, sir. Why now? What's the story on this?"

"No story, Sergeant. Or shall I say 'Lieutenant'? The Army rewards its own—it's that simple."

By george, Goodman had human qualities after all. But my expression must have changed as he continued:

"You will be the Medical Administrative Officer on one of three ships—I can't tell you which one at this time—and one more year is the only price tag."

So there it was, the worm in the apple. I didn't buy the package, if for no other reason than my distrust of the salesperson. I did try to be courteous. I explained that Major Freund had encouraged me to study medicine, that I had begun accumulating college credits as a pre-med student under the USAFI program some months back, and that I had already enrolled at IU for the summer semester.

None of this phased Lt. Goodman. He was hard-sell all the way, Finally, after ten minutes of listening to his pitch, I lost patience, and did what I had cautioned myself not to do, and said what I should not have said: I told him in what part of his anatomy he could stuff the commission.

Understandably, the lieutenant was not pleased, and there was a certain gleam in his eye when I was dismissed which I knew boded ill. For the next eleven days I waited for my orders . . . and waited . . . and waited. Men around me in the dormitory would come in one day and depart the following day. But day after day no orders for me. I was far too proud to go crawling back to Lt. Goodman. Instead I went to the operations office and volunteered for work detail.

A medic's swan song

The Army never turns down a volunteer. The next morning a new recruit and I were directed to report to a place on the Hudson River north of New York City called Camp Shanks Landing. We were assigned an Army ambulance, and I drove, because my little buddy said he was scared of city traffic (he hailed from a place called "Bean Station, Tennessee"). Our job was simply to stand by on the pier as German prisoners of war were loaded on Victory ships to be sent home.

But it turned out to be not so simple. A wave of Army trucks loaded with prisoners came barreling up at an incredible rate of speed. The first truck in line came within five feet of running off the pier into the Hudson River. The driver leaped out, and there was total confusion as I tried to make sense of the soldier's disjointed phrases, and the babble of thirty-five Germans gathered around us all talking at once.

When I got the gist of it, my little buddy clung to the dashboard panel as we raced the ambulance back to the barracks where the men had been confined. There we found two German prisoners hanging, side by side, from a ceiling beam.

I stepped up on the bench they had used as a scaffold and listened for heartbeats, but, of course, we were much too late. No Camp Shanks official had appeared yet, so I spoke in garbled German and English with a prisoner who had been waiting outside the baracks. He said the dead men had lived in what was now the Russian zone of East Germany. They had been getting mail from surviving members of their families, and the news of brutal treatment of the Germans by the Russians filled the pages. As the day of repatriation approached, they had become more and more despondent, and finally made the decision to end it all, rather than face life under Russian occupation. Perhaps they had special reasons for being apprehensive, special reasons for fearing the Russians, who knows? In any event, I waited until the camp authorities arrived before we got them down, and that was my last official act as an Army medic.

The end of the line

After waiting for ten long days I figured something had to have happened to my papers. I decided a bottle of Canadian Velvet donated to a master sergeant would be money well spent, and it was. The sergeant searched Goodman's desk during lunch break, and in the last place he looked, on the bottom of Goodman's junk drawer, there it lay—my file, with my orders. Those eleven days of waiting as a consequence of my untoward remark should have taught me a lesson to last the rest of my life about controlling my Irish temper, but I'm afraid I've made the same mistake more than once since then.

Nevertheless, I think I would have given my severance pay to hear what Goodman's comments were when he discovered his bird had flown the coop.

But of course the bird didn't fly—he took the New York Central train on the travel voucher the Army supplied. I watched the increasingly familiar landscape we passed with escalating anticipation of the homecoming that awaited. The trip seemed unending. In western Ohio to vary the monotony, I changed seats. I had been facing forward, but I switched to a seat facing to the rear, since the train was relatively uncrowded and no one was sitting there. At Lawrence, Indiana, I was dozing—another fifty miles and I'd be at Camp Atterbury, where I would be converted into a civilian again.

Suddenly, I heard a loud explosion, and something sharp struck my face. There was a thudding sound against the seat across from me where I had been ensconced before. I looked around and discovered the double-paned window was gone—the heavy aluminum frame had an ugly gouged-out place at about the height of a seated man's head. I glanced down then and saw that my uniform was covered with powdered glass. Then I saw the porter lying face down in the aisle atop a mess of pillows he had been carrying towards the rear of the coach.

I thought he had been wounded so I jumped over the pillows and kneeled down to examine him. He was looking up at me, his eyes wide with terror, and shaking convulsively.

"Are you hit?" I asked.

"Naw, suh! I ain't, I don' think. But, Lawdy, you is!"

He was gazing fixedly at my face, so I put my hand up and adjusted my eyeglasses, which were still in place. I got some bloody smudges on my fingers, but nothing alarming.

By this time the train had screeched to a halt. Some minutes later the conductor entered the car and asked me to step outside with him. There coming up onto the berm were several sheriff's deputies, herding in front of them a group of unlikely assassins. One of the officers was carrying the gun, a 22-caliber rifle and a handful of cartridges. Two of the culprits were wailing loudly, and a third was giving his fingernails a good biting. I don't suppose any of them had reached his tenth birthday yet.

I listened as they sobbed out the story of the "game" they were playing, called "shoot at the train."

The two officers who seemed to be in charge approached and asked if I needed medical attention. I said I didn't seem to be hurt. Then they wanted to know if I intended to press charges against the boys. I remembered, then, a time many years ago on a summer evening when I had flung a stone at a chimney outlined against the night sky, missed, and hit Mrs. Tague's front window instead. No one had put me in jail . . .

So I said, "Why don't you have their parents come pick these little fellows up, tell them what happened, and let them decide on the punishment."

They nodded, and I reboarded the train. When I got back into the coach an officer had just fished the slug from the seat opposite mine.

"Good thing no one was sitting here, " he said, "or he would have been killed."

Yes, I thought, but someone *was* sitting there just a few minutes ago. The irony of the occasion struck me forcibly then: nineteen crossings of the Atlantic, and killed a few miles from home by some little boys playing a "game." I guess the good Lord never intended for me to be a hero.

We got into Union Station in Indianapolis and I went to the washroom to clean up. Now I understood why people had been staring at me. Except for the circles where my glasses had been I was covered with thousands of tiny dots of blood from the powdered glass. But it looked worse than it was.

I got through most of the red tape at Camp Atterbury with dispatch. Then I was told to go into a theater with some comfortable seats where a couple of dozen men were waiting for a movie to be shown. They were in scattered groups, talking quietly.

I heard names and phrases casually mentioned, "Bloody Ridge . . . Iwo . . . Saipan . . . Truk . . ." And "Oran . . . Sidi Barrani . . . St. Lo. . . . Kasserine Pass . . . Bastogne . . . Ploesti . . . Omaha . . . Remagen."

I sort of dug deeper in my seat. I was out of place. These were some of the *heroes* who had lived to tell the tale.

An amiable Army captain with plenty of salad on his left chest entered and waved down scattered attempts of some of us to rise, in accordance with military courtesy. He was a real salesman! The military was desperately trying to keep the ranks from being depleted, I guess, because he had a file on every man in the room. His presentation was so persuasive that by the time we had seen the movie and he had finished talking, at least ten per cent of those present had agreed to go to a further meeting. But I didn't. I had other plans for my future.

Just before the meeting was over the captain asked me to wait and meet with him afterwards. When I was sitting across from him in his office he flashed a form showing that some colonel had filled out a request for my return to Brooke General in San Antonio upon re-enlistment.

I told him I appreciated the colonel's vote of confidence and his interest, but wanted to proceed with the plans I had already made. But I recall wishing my dad could see that document. I had carried a monkey on my back all during the war after making the decision to volunteer.

Unlike many youngsters today, I did indeed "give a damn" what my parents thought of me and my actions.

"Robby, you're a damn fool," my father had said then. "One more man isn't going to make any difference."

Well, I wasn't a hero like some of those fellows, but I do believe my father was wrong that one time—I think I did, at least, make a difference.

The Queen *with tenders alongside.*

THE *QUEEN'S* VITAL STATISTICS

Builders: John Brown & Co., Ltd., Clydebank, Scotland
Keel Laid: December 1, 1930
Maiden Voyage: May 27—June 1, 1936
Overall length: 1,019'6"
Fastest speed: 31.69 knots
Number of Decks: 12
Passenger Capacity: 1,957 persons
Number of Cabins: 949
Officers & Crew: 1,174 full complement
Lifeboats: 24, each with 145 person capacity
Funnels: Last of the three-funneled ships
Bridge: 90 feet above waterline

THE *QUEEN'S* WAR HISTORY

August 30—September 4, 1939 — Carried record number of civilian passengers (2,239) mostly U.S. citizens leaving Europe as war threatened.

March 21, 1940 — Left New York for Sydney, Australia to be outfitted as a troop ship.

1940-1942 Sailed to England with Australian troops, ferried troops between England and Middle East, and between Australia and Egypt/Middle East.

1942 — ("40 Days, 40 Nights Voyage") Left Boston February 18, 1942; sailed to Key West to Rio to Capetown to Fremantle to Sydney, arriving March 28, 1942; carried 905 Cunard crew and 8,398 American troops to serve in the Pacific theater.

1942-1943 — Shuttled between Australia and Middle East, and between U.S. and Scotland.

1943-1945 — Shuttled between New York and Scotland carrying American troops to Great Britain and returning with wounded, prisoners of war, and rotation troops; after V-J Day transported 5,000 European POWs who had been interned in Asia from New York to England, and 12,886 GI brides and children from England to U.S.

1940-1946 — Transported 765,429 military personnel 569,943 miles. Transported Winston Churchill and his staff three times during war for conferences in U.S. and Canada.